MW00697247

A PARENT'S GUIDE TO

Sorrow & Suffering

@CHRISTIANPARENTING_ORG

@CHRISTIANPARENTING.ORG

CHRISTIANPARENTING.COM

© 2020 Christian Parenting
All rights reserved.
All Scripture quotations, unless otherwise indicated, are taken from the Holy Bible, New International Version®,
NIV®. Copyright ©1973, 1978, 1984, 2011 by Biblica, Inc.™ Used by permission of Zondervan. All rights reserved
worldwide. www.zondervan.com The "NIV" and "New International Version" are trademarks registered in the
United States Patent and Trademark Office by Biblica, Inc.™

Scripture quotations marked (ESV) are from The ESV® Bible (The Holy Bible, English Standard Version®), copyright
© 2001 by Crossway, a publishing ministry of Good News Publishers. Used by permission. All rights reserved.

A PARENT'S GUIDE TO

Sorrow & Suffering

DANIEL AND KELLY CRAWFORD

CHRISTIAN PARENTING

Table of
Contents

DANIEL AND KELLY CRAWFORD HAVE BEEN MARRIED SINCE DECEMBER 2013 AND RESIDE IN DALLAS, TEXAS.

They have three children (Abel, Mayfield, and Deacon) who were all born on the exact same day in 2016, 2017, and 2019. Yes, January 22 is a big day at the Crawford house!

They co-founded Abel Speaks in 2018 to support families who have chosen to carry a child with a life-limiting diagnosis. After walking that road with their firstborn son, Abel, they realized the significant need that existed for parents in their position.

The vision of Abel Speaks is that every family they serve will cherish their child's life and have hope in the midst of sorrow. This ministry is but one example of the redemptive truth that God never wastes an ounce of our pain, and the Crawfords love to write and speak on the ways that God can and does use our suffering for his glory and our good.

GO TO ABELSPEAKS.ORG TO FIND OUT MORE.

IT ALL STARTED IN AN AIRPORT

It was January of 2012, and we were in Fort Myers, Florida. We prepared to board a plane to Port au Prince where we would live for the next five months when we locked eyes and started a conversation. Let's just say it didn't take a science lab to discover pretty quickly that there was some "chemistry" going on between the two of us. Despite the company policy that mandated that interns were not allowed to date one another, we found a way to grow a friendship and then a relationship—don't tell anybody! Roll the tape forward 23 months, and we were married on December 1, 2013.

Even if you don't know much else about Haiti, you probably remember hearing about the catastrophic earthquake that struck in January of 2010. It left a beautiful nation, already too familiar with suffering, in complete devastation. As Kelly and I lived among and labored alongside Haitians following this tragedy, we would come to witness this daily struggle with sorrow and suffering in new ways. It was painful, powerful, and personal. Little did we know how this season would also lay the groundwork for what was to come for us just a couple of years later.

For that, I'll pass the pen over to Kelly.

OUR FIRSTBORN SON

It was a Monday morning during the summer of 2015 when we received a call that our genetic testing results had come in. We discovered that our first child was a boy. And then, seconds later, we discovered that our little boy was conceived with an extra 18th chromosome; a life-limiting abnormality known as Trisomy 18. Nothing could have prepared us for that moment. Our world came crashing down, the future we envisioned with our child began slipping away.

SO RATHER THAN GIVING OUR LITTLE BOY AN ABORTION, WE GAVE HIM A NAME.

We were brand-new parents, and suddenly we had to come to grips with the reality that our baby's life would more than likely be short if his diagnosis held true.

We were encouraged to terminate the pregnancy and try again for a "better" one—which was to say, a healthier one. We understand the mixed emotions surrounding this choice that parents are offered. But if our son's death was impending, we decided we would not be the ones to set that date. So rather than giving our little boy an abortion, we gave him a name. Abel Paul Crawford's beautiful and unconventional journey on earth continued.

CONTINUED

Not knowing how long that journey would last, we received an unexpected gift. We didn't take a single day for granted, savoring each and every one of them. Every kick in my tummy. Every sonogram. Every week watching my belly grow in accordance with my son's body. I carried him for thirty-nine weeks, and Abel was born on January 22, 2016. We were given the honor of loving and taking care of him for fifteen days outside of the womb.

JOY AND SUFFERING

As odd as it sounds, we can honestly tell you that our time with Abel was simultaneously the happiest and the saddest, the best and the hardest thirty-nine weeks and fifteen days of our lives. In some ways, people may think it would have been easier for us to choose the other route. But the truth is, terminating our son would not have spared us an ounce of loss or despair. It would have only robbed us of the joyful memories that forever mark our season with Abel.

Along the way, we've learned that joy and suffering are not mutually exclusive. In fact, the deep pain we feel from losing Abel is directly and inseparably tied to the pure joy we had in knowing and loving him fully. No restraint. No regrets. However imperfectly we've done

> AS WE WALK WITH PARENTS THROUGH THE VALLEY OF THE SHADOW OF DEATH, ABEL SPEAKS IS BUT ONE EXAMPLE OF THE REDEMPTIVE TRUTH THAT GOD NEVER WASTES AN OUNCE OF OUR PAIN.

it, stewarding Abel's life has been the single greatest privilege of ours.

We chose to embrace a different story than the one we had planned, and we found that it is possible to navigate this broken world with a redemptive perspective in the midst of life's many challenges. Through Abel's life, the story we dreamed of was replaced with a greater one—a harder one no doubt, but a greater one. Hebrews 11:4 says, "And by faith Abel still speaks, even though he is dead." The ways Abel has changed us are incalculable. But, in one of the most practical ways, his story has changed our calling and our vocation.

NOTHING IS WASTED

It became painfully clear to us in the months following our time with Abel that the vast majority of families in our situation were either choosing termination or simply enduring their child's story rather than embracing and enjoying it. On January 22, 2018, what would have been Abel's second birthday, Abel Speaks was officially born: a nonprofit organization we founded to better support families who choose to carry a child with a life-limiting diagnosis during pregnancy. And I would be remiss if I didn't mention that our daughter Mayfield was born on January 22, 2017, and our son Deacon was born on January 22, 2019—Yeah, you can't make this stuff up!

At Abel Speaks, it is our vision that every family we serve will cherish their child's life and have hope in the midst of sorrow. As we walk with parents through the valley of the shadow of death, Abel Speaks is but one example of the redemptive truth that God never wastes an ounce of our pain. He can take our mess and turn it into a message for a world that never knew how badly they needed it. If our eyes are open to it, we will see that Jesus gives us vision in the valley and strength for the next step. One step at a time.

Introduction

Where do you find yourself today?

We're at a slight disadvantage here. We've just had the privilege of sharing a little bit of our backstory with you, but we haven't the faintest idea of where this workbook finds you. Given that "sorrow and suffering" is in the title, we are writing with the assumption that this season has not been the best or easiest for you. Whether you are walking through hardship or you are witnessing its impact on your children, your family, or your friends, we are so very sorry.

Before we dive headlong into this conversation, I figured we should try to frame and define this word that can bring so much to mind for so many people: *suffering*. If we used the good ol' dictionary as a starting point, we would read that suffering is "the state of undergoing pain, distress, or hardship." With that said, we would hate it if you felt like the challenging circumstances that led you to pick up this book somehow failed to "qualify" as suffering. It would be a great shame to invalidate whatever it is that drove you to open these pages. The fact that this workbook has found its way into your hands clearly validates at least one thing: God is pursuing you in your pain and inviting you to seek him in return.

So I'd like to supplement the dictionary with a definition from Elisabeth Elliott. In her words from *A Path Through Suffering,* "suffering is having what you don't want or wanting what you don't have." I think it's fair to say that the experience of parenting itself comes with about a thousand things that fit that bill, and it's okay to acknowledge and articulate those areas of our life where we are left wanting.

THREE UNIVERSAL REALITIES

While there's so much we *don't* know about your specific circumstances, there are at least three universal realities we *do* know about the human experience as it relates to suffering. No matter who you are, these are truths that apply to us all.

1. **Suffering is something we will all experience at one time or another and in one way or another.** You're either currently in a season of suffering, you've recently been through one, or you'll be entering into one soon enough. (Fun pep talk, huh?)

2. **Suffering is something we are hard-wired to try and avoid, at all costs.** From the physiological reactions in our body to the ways we consciously seek safety and security, our "default mode" is to pursue pleasure and avoid pain.

3. **Suffering is something that can lead to our growth (and therefore our good) in a way that nothing else can.** The Scriptures have a *ton* to say about this, and therefore, so will we. It's an absolutely pivotal truth that we will point back to often as we strive to unpack a biblical, redemptive perspective on suffering.

The reality is that even if we knew exactly what you were going through, most of the time there truly are no perfect words to say. And that makes writing a workbook for parents on the topic of suffering a pretty tall task, so we do hope you'll extend grace as we put forth our best effort in the weeks ahead.

We don't pretend to be "suffering experts" and we don't expect a four-week study to "fix" all that is broken, but it is our sincere hope and prayer that this workbook might serve as a helpful resource to you in the midst of this hard season. And it is our sincere hope that you, too, will come to learn that joy and suffering are not mutually exclusive.

In this with you,

Daniel & Kelly Crawford

How to
use this
workbook

5 DAYS A WEEK

SHORT LESSON

DISCUSSION QUESTIONS

GUIDED PRAYER

NOTES

Over the next month, we will continue to share stories, verses, quotes, and other reflections. We will aim to address aspects of sorrow and suffering with as broad of brush strokes as possible while also striving to offer practical handle-holds and questions for you to process and discuss day by day.

If you are married, we hope that this will be a journey you both take together. The goal is to help you feel practically and spiritually equipped to walk this road of suffering with God, but this workbook is also meant to bring you two closer together as a couple and a team. The daily challenge is to keep your hearts soft and your communication lines open as you make your way through these next four weeks.

In this workbook, we will cover some of the highest-felt needs of this hard season:

Week 1: Wrestling with God

Week 2: Myths & truths

Week 3: Relational roadblocks

Week 4: Purpose in the pain

Our prayer is for this experience to be so much more about the process than the destination. This is not about simply completing the lessons, but allowing the content to help you see your circumstances and your very selves with fresh eyes and fresh hearts.

With that said, for all you scorekeepers out there, I'll throw out four metrics for you. This workbook will fulfill its aim and this commitment will have been a success if:

1. **You have grown in your own personal self-awareness,** having processed thoughts and feelings that have gone unexpressed or unexplored.

2. **You have a greater mutual understanding** and a deeper connection with your spouse, having walked and talked through your sufferings together.

3. **You realize that your pain is never pointless,** having embraced the fact that God can (and does) use it for his glory and our good.

4. **You are experiencing daily intimacy with Jesus Christ,** having found the Man of Sorrows more relevant and more relatable than ever before.

We are honored to play the guide as we walk through this next month together. I promise your brave commitment, investment, and self-discipline will not be in vain.

Let's take a step together!

1

WEEK ONE

WRESTLING WITH GOD

"

...you may feel like wrestling with God is the antithesis of faith in God.

What does it mean to truly "have faith"? It seems like somewhere in our spiritual journeys, we have either internally assumed or been explicitly taught that struggling or questioning God in any way is akin to blasphemy. In other words, you may feel like wrestling with God is the antithesis of faith in God. If this describes you in any way, we'd like to offer a different perspective at the outset of this workbook. While faith is required, it is very different from blind conformity and compliance. In fact, I daresay any religious establishment that discourages seeking and asking honest, heartfelt questions about their beliefs ought to concern you. So let's go to the heart of the Scriptures and see how God seems to view the reality of struggling, questioning, and wrestling that occurs in our human hearts.

WHAT WE SEE IN SCRIPTURE

The book of Psalms is a collection of Hebrew poetry to be meditated upon, prayed through, and sung together as God's people. You can think of it like a 150-song playlist designed to honor and worship God. And yet, interestingly enough, as you read through these poems, you'll notice that the reflections and sentiments they express are all over the place. But to over-simplify, you will find two broad categories: psalms of praise and psalms of lament. I'm pointing this out because throughout these worship songs, you will find unbelievable joy, unspeakable suffering, and everything in between. This is really important.

Humans are relational creatures, and humans are emotional creatures. The good news is that God knows and understands this; he designed and created us this way. So why do we suddenly feel like we have to hide or manage these emotions from him? The psalmists sure didn't seem to pull any punches. As you read through them, you will see worshippers of God being completely honest with how they are feeling—like really, brutally, teenage-indie-music honest with him. "My tears have been my food day and night" (Psalm 42:3). Yikes.

And guess what? God seems to be completely comfortable and okay with this. His Holy Spirit didn't hesitate to capture and preserve these sentiments in the Holy Scriptures. I hope it is relieving or even liberating for you to know that the worship hymnal of the ancient people of God is chock-full of poetry from faithful followers who struggled, grappled, and wrestled with God. And just to clarify, the psalms are not unique in this. You can observe it from Jesus and the apostles all the way back to the first book of the Bible, where a man literally wrestles with God before having his name changed to "Israel" (ring a bell?) which means, "wrestles with God." An entire nation named and built upon this premise! Look it up, I'm serious.

It seems as though there is a healthy way to humbly and honestly wrestle with God. I believe that ultimately, these worshippers aren't so much fighting him as they are fighting to cling to him and his truth in the midst of life's ups and downs. That's what I hope we can begin to do together in the days and weeks ahead.

FIVE HONEST QUESTIONS

As we move ahead into Week 1, we will address a handful of the most common and fundamental questions we often face while undergoing suffering. In Week 2, we will get into some of the prevailing "answers" that worldly wisdom has to offer, and discover that many of the most common explanations are unbiblical at best and absolutely destructive at worst.

For now, let's begin by taking an honest look at some honest questions.

WHAT IS HAPPENING?

"But sometimes a loss cuts into your heart so viciously that it forever redefines who you are and how you think. It's what I call 'deep grief.' The kind that strains against everything you've ever believed. So much so you wonder how the promises that seemed so real on those thin Bible pages yesterday could possibly ever stand up under the weight of this enormous sadness today." —Lysa TerKeurst, Deep Grief

"Why do bad things happen to good and innocent people? If God is all-powerful and all-loving, why is there so much suffering in the world?" This question in its various forms has come to be known as "the problem of evil and suffering." As people struggle to reconcile the fundamental attributes of God with their painful experiences, this "problem" remains one of the biggest obstacles to a trusting faith in a sovereign God.

THE PROBLEM OF EVIL & SUFFERING

Often the tension of this question will be tackled from an intellectual vantage point, sparking a robust philosophical conversation while puffing on a Gandalf-like tobacco pipe. (At least, that's how it plays out in my head.) However, after spending significant time and effort equipping myself intellectually, I've come to find that this question doesn't pack its full punch in the form of apologetics or late-night debates.

SCRIPTURE

"I say to God my Rock, 'Why have you forgotten me? Why must I go about mourning, oppressed by the enemy?' My bones suffer mortal agony as my foes taunt me, saying to me all day long, 'Where is your God?'" —Psalm 42:9–10

When people truly begin to wrestle with the issue of human suffering, it is not primarily at a head level; *it is at a heart level.* The question is not so much about why God permits painful things to happen in the world, but why God permits painful things to happen *in my world* and the world of those I love. For most of us, it is far more emotional than philosophical. I highly doubt that you picked up this workbook in an attempt to explain God's action or inaction on a rational level; I imagine most of us are primarily and deeply hurting on a *personal* level.

NOT WHAT I EXPECTED

Our aim in this first week of exploration is not to try and sprint toward resolution or figure out the "answers." For now, I think a helpful first step is acknowledging something at a very foundational level: *you are grieving.*

There are literally hundreds of books about grief, but in this one we really just want to say one thing: at its core, grief is coming face-to-face with the reality that life is going to look different than you thought. Our grieving didn't begin when Abel passed away in his mother's arms on February 6, 2016. It began the previous summer with that Monday morning phone call and all of its implications.

It is impossible to overstate the power of the unspoken and unrealized expectations we all carry with us. I wonder how much of the persisting pain we feel is closely tied to this sentiment: *"This looks a whole lot different than I thought. This isn't what I wanted for my life. It's not supposed to be this way."* Much of the devastation we feel stems from having never envisioned that this would possibly become a part of our stories. And we need to grieve that.

AT ITS CORE, GRIEF IS COMING FACE-TO-FACE WITH THE REALITY THAT LIFE IS GOING TO LOOK DIFFERENT THAN YOU THOUGHT.

SEEMINGLY SENSELESS SUFFERING

There have been hardships in my life where I'm able to clearly connect the dots from a painful consequence back to a regrettable decision or action. While it didn't make it easy, at least I could wrap my mind around what was happening. But sometimes, our suffering just seems senseless. It doesn't seem fair, and it doesn't make sense. It leaves us crushed and confused.

"Suffering in its simplest form comes in the space between what we thought would be and what is."
—Jay and Katherine Wolf, Suffer Strong: How to Survive Anything by Redefining Everything

A fluke accident.

A miscarriage.

A debilitating disease.

A natural disaster.

A prodigal child.

An unexpected loss.

A chromosomal abnormality, in our case.

It is normal and it is okay to put words to the fact that you cannot understand why God would permit such unforeseeable and unexplainable hands to be dealt. *"Why me? Why is this happening? Where is God in all of this? Will this ever end?"*

The difficult reality is that we may never have our deepest questions answered on this side of eternity. But while there are certain things we may never know, there is much that has been revealed to us. The word of God speaks volumes. And while the Bible may not always resolve questions of "Why?", its pages absolutely reverberate with proclamations of "Who!" That's where we're headed tomorrow as we begin to explore the character and nature of this God with whom we are wrestling.

1. **Start this week by giving yourselves the freedom to put some honest words on what you are feeling at a heart level, perhaps for the very first time.** *"I am grieving. This is not what I expected. I am angry. This is not what I wanted. I don't understand."*

2. **What aspect of "the problem of evil" do you have the hardest time with?** What are the main areas where you find yourselves wrestling with God right now?

3. **Is this your first time walking through a season marked by suffering?** If not, what have these seasons of wrestling with God been like for you in the past both individually and as a couple?

4. **What are some of the ways that your life and circumstances currently look different than you had hoped or envisioned?** In other words, what are you grieving? We would invite you to put honest and specific words on these, and then we would encourage you to share them with each other.

1. **Take a moment to acknowledge** and articulate to God what is heaviest on your heart right now.

2. **If you can do so genuinely, invite God to help you trust him even in the absence of answers.** If you're not there yet, pray that the days and weeks ahead will help move you closer to that and closer to him.

3. **Personalize and pray the following,** and feel encouraged to add anything else that you'd like to tell God. If you feel comfortable doing so, you could hold hands and do this together.

God, there's so much we just don't understand.

In the coming weeks, help us to seek you and to see you.

Thank you for inviting and giving us the space to wrestle with hard things.

While so much is foggy, give us a clearer picture of who you are.

We humbly ask you to begin healing our hurting hearts.

One day at a time.

Amen.

WHO IS GOD?

"Awake, Lord! Why do you sleep? Rouse yourself! Do not reject us forever. Why do you hide your face and forget our misery and oppression?" —Psalm 44:23–24

"The eyes of the Lord are on the righteous, and his ears are attentive to their cry . . . The righteous cry out, and the Lord hears them; he delivers them from all their troubles. The Lord is close to the brokenhearted and saves those who are crushed in spirit." —Psalm 34:15–18

"The Israelites groaned in their slavery and cried out . . . God *heard* their groaning and he *remembered* his covenant with Abraham, with Isaac, and with Jacob. So God looked on the Israelites and was *concerned* about them." —Exodus 2:23–25, emphasis added

As we move ahead in this first week, I want to continue leaning into the big "Why?" questions while slowly and simultaneously steering toward a deeper and more personal question: "Who is this God of the Bible, and what is he like?"

WHAT COMES TO YOUR MIND?

Among many profoundly complex things that A. W. Tozer wrote over the course of his life, he made one claim in *The Knowledge of the Holy* that is profoundly simple and yet incredibly bold. He said, "What comes into our minds when we think about God is the most important thing about us." Dang. I never met A. W. Tozer, but I did meet Adam Tarnow, a dear mentor of mine who built a sermon around this concept where he summarized some of the more stereotypical (and misguided) views of God in our day. If you'll indulge me for a moment, I think it helps illustrate the far-reaching implications of Tozer's claim.

Star Wars God: A mighty Force that is clearly powerful but not so personal.

Chipotle God: We get to pick and choose what we like and dismiss what we don't.

JESUS WANTS US TO HAVE A CLEAR VIEW
OF OUR CREATOR AND APPROACH HIM
FOR WHO HE TRULY IS AND ALWAYS WILL
BE—*FATHER GOD*.

Scoreboard God: Clipboard in hand, he is watching closely and waiting for us to fall short.

Siri God: We ask for him when there's a problem to solve or a request to be made.

Grandpa God: He's sweet, he's wise, and he's a little out of touch in the 21st century.

President God: He's in charge but busy dealing with issues bigger than mine.

I'm sure you could add to this list, but I think you get the point. When a person hears the word *God*, there are dozens of things that may come to mind, right or wrong. With all of those different options and impressions, wouldn't it be helpful if we were given an accurate and definitive view from the Scriptures— maybe even straight from the mouth of Jesus? Well friends, in a week full of daunting questions, here is one occasion where we're given a straight answer.

WHAT CAME TO JESUS' MIND

There is one single word that Jesus uses 180 times in the Gospels to address, describe, and communicate about who God is and what he is like: *Abba*. No, not the cheesy Swedish pop group. The closest translation from Hebrew to English is the word *daddy*. It is a childlike, intimate term for a loving father. Jesus wants us to have a clear view of our Creator and approach him for who he truly is and always will be—*Father God*.

Long before the ministry of Jesus, the book of Exodus is where God really begins to reveal himself to a broken man named Moses and then to a rescued and redeemed people at the foot of Mount Sinai. It is here that we're introduced to the personal description of God that the biblical authors would go on to quote and reference repeatedly: "The Lord, the Lord, the compassionate and gracious God, slow to anger, abounding in love and faithfulness, maintaining love to thousands, and forgiving wickedness, rebellion, and sin" (Exodus 34:6–7).

Compassionate. Gracious. Loving. Faithful. Forgiving. This is who God the Father is.

God is not just there when you have a request—he's with you constantly.

God is not outdated and irrelevant—he offers us abundant life, now and forever.

God is not distant and disinterested—he knows you by name and he cares for you.

God is not an impersonal force—he's a loving, patient, and faithful father to his kids.

SO THEN, WHERE IS THIS HEAVENLY FATHER OF MINE?

If we know the picture we ought to have in mind as we think about God, that's certainly a helpful step. But that doesn't instantly take our present pain away, does it? In fact, for many of us reflecting back from childhood up to the present, "father" might be the single worst word Jesus could have picked. And if that is the case for you, then I am so sorry. Regardless of the relationship we have with our earthly fathers, in times of deep suffering, it can feel as though our Heavenly Father is absent, indifferent, negligent, harsh, or even downright abusive. It's easy to wrestle with the question, *"Where is God in the midst of this?"* His apparent silence conjures up the painful picture of a child desperately scanning the crowd or calling out for an attentive parent, but met with . . . nothing. Abandoned. Vulnerable. Scared. Alone.

"When we cannot understand the mind of God, we remind ourselves of what we do know about Him. And often that comes about by looking at the ways He has provided in the past." —Ashlee Profitt, The Morning, "Christmas Hope for the Grieving Mom"

After putting words on the fake IDs we attribute to God, Adam would then say, "God is not the reflection of your earthly father. He is the perfection of your earthly father." Our Father God is never abusive, nor is He ever absent—even when our human experiences seem to scream otherwise. We see the biblical authors wrestle and struggle and question—and then they remind themselves of God's heart and his perfect track record of faithfulness through the highs and the lows (and you can read for yourself, they had themselves some *lows*). And then the craziest thing happens; they push pause on the fighting, and they find their rest in him. One day at a time.

He sees you and he cares about you. He has not left you, and he has not forgotten you. In each and every season, he is *with* you and he is *for* you. He is a good, good Father.

GOD IS NOT THE REFLECTION OF YOUR EARTHLY FATHER. HE IS THE *PERFECTION* OF YOUR EARTHLY FATHER.

1. **When you think of God, what do you imagine?** Did any of those false examples resonate with your view of him in the past or present? Discuss with each other what images you both have.

2. **Take time to talk about your earthly fathers.** Does that help you to see your Heavenly Father in a better or worse light? What's the hardest thing for you both to believe about God as a father in this season of suffering?

3. **Has there ever been a moment where you truly felt God's nearness?** What was it about that moment that made him feel so present and real to you? In what other ways have you experienced God's faithfulness in your life?

1. **Reread these core characteristics of God** given to us in Exodus 34: compassionate, gracious, loving, faithful, and forgiving. Take a moment to meditate on each one of those words.

2. **Acknowledge the faulty and worldly perceptions** you've believed about God. Invite him to shape your view and soften your heart to know him for who he truly is.

3. **Personalize and pray the following,** and feel encouraged to add anything else that you'd like to tell God. If you feel comfortable doing so, you could hold hands and do this together.

Father in Heaven,

You are compassionate, gracious, and slow to anger.

You abound in love and faithfulness.

You forgive wickedness, rebellion, and sin.

Thank you for making me your child, and for being to me a perfect, loving Father.

When we cannot trace your hand, please help us to trust your heart.

One day at a time.

Amen.

WHY PRAY TO GOD?

SCRIPTURE

"You, Lord, hear the desire of the afflicted; you encourage them, and you listen to their cry, defending the fatherless and the oppressed."
—Psalm 10:17–18

"In the same way, the Spirit helps us in our weakness. We do not know what we ought to pray for, but the Spirit himself intercedes for us through wordless groans. And he who searches our hearts knows the mind of the Spirit, because the Spirit intercedes for God's people in accordance with the will of God. And we know that in all things God works for the good of those who love him, who have been called according to his purpose."
—Romans 8:26–28

Have you ever heard of the "friend zone"? It's when one friend is interested in the other, but that pursuit goes unreciprocated. You boldly approach someone you care for and share that you have feelings for them, all to end up feeling denied and dismissed when you don't get the response you were hoping for. Eventually, to avoid repeated discouragement, you just stop asking. You're stuck in the friend zone.

I start there because millions and millions of people have wrestled with a similar sentiment in relation to prayer. We share our heart with our Heavenly Father, only to find that our prayers don't seem to "work" the way that we hope they would and think they should. Over time, fatigue sets in. We get tired of feeling stiff-armed or ignored. Intentionally or unintentionally, we resign ourselves to a life of prayerlessness.

WHEN GOD "DOESN'T ANSWER"

There are a couple of assumptions we are prone to make about prayer. Most notably, we are often quick to assume that we know what is best in a given situation. We never say it quite like this, but we often conclude, "If I was all-powerful God, I'd certainly answer these specific prayers in these specific ways." When a prayer doesn't get answered the way we were expecting or hoping, it can make us wonder, *If he hears me and cares for me, and if he can respond to these specific requests, why on earth would he choose not to?*

What that string of logic fails to humbly consider is that God has a completely different vantage point. "'For my thoughts are not your thoughts, neither are your ways my ways,' declares the Lord" (Isaiah 55:8). We are also quick to assume that our prayers are "unanswered" unless they come to fruition fully and precisely as prayed. In reality, God can absolutely answer a prayer request by saying, "I love you, but no," or, "not right now." Every parent knows this to be true. In his book titled *Prayer*, Tim Keller writes, "God will either give us what we ask for in prayer, or he will give us what we *would have* asked for if we knew everything he knew" (emphasis added).

In the midst of deep suffering, that statement may feel insensitive or even insulting, which is obviously not Keller's intent in writing it or ours in sharing it. Personally, we would never have willfully asked for our son's life to be short, nor could we bring ourselves to pray for such a thing today. And yet, as time rolls on, it is absolutely amazing to watch the ripple effects of Abel's story going forth. In mysterious ways very different from what we'd ever ask for, God is at work behind the scenes. Powerfully, indescribably, and undeniably at work.

In fact, many of the greatest blessings in my life have flowed from God answering prayers very differently than I asked. I bet you can think back and say the same. God absolutely hears every request from his children, and he is absolutely committed to graciously answering them with a yes, no, or a not yet. When you begin to believe that his heart, his ways, and his timing can all be trusted through thick and thin, the stage becomes set for him to wow you with the unexpected. When you see the Lord come through powerfully and even *differently* than you asked or knew to ask for, it is an extremely faith-inducing experience.

"God didn't give me the physical healing I had wanted, but the deeper healing I needed so much more. Maybe your prayer has been, 'God, why won't you remove my problem? Why won't you change my situation? Why won't you heal me—from this pain, this sickness, this struggle, this disability?' The fact is, he might! He might remove that 'thorn in your flesh' and sooner than you think. But in the meantime, he might also use that suffering to draw you closer to his heart, shaping and forming you for purposes beyond your imagination." —Joni Eareckson Tada, *Beside Bethesda*

GOD ABSOLUTELY HEARS EVERY REQUEST FROM HIS CHILDREN,
AND HE IS ABSOLUTELY COMMITTED TO GRACIOUSLY
ANSWERING THEM WITH A YES, NO, OR A NOT YET.

SO THEN, WHAT'S THE POINT?

All of that begs the question, *What is the purpose of prayer?* If God's going to do what he's going to do and I can trust him in that, then why bother praying in the first place? When prayer is primarily just the means by which we persuade our Creator to change our circumstances, we will quickly and inevitably become disillusioned and disappointed. But what if prayer is not simply a means to a desired end? If true, this could change everything about how, why, and when we pray.

We would contend that *the primary purpose of prayer is intimacy with God.* We would also contend that it is in the lowest valleys that we can personally and prayerfully experience the deepest intimacy with God. We have often seen that the people who have suffered the worst seem to be the ones who end up knowing God the best. Much like the questions we are exploring and wrestling with this week, that statement really doesn't make sense, and yet it is so.

In those places of deep sorrow, we can encounter the Man of Sorrows himself and profoundly connect with him as we share in his sufferings. In *A Story Unfinished*, Matt Mooney powerfully summarizes this truth as he writes, "You can know God more, even if you understand him less." Our prayer is that you would see personal intimacy with God as the chief aim of your prayers, and that it might transform your perspective as you approach the Lord in this season of suffering and beyond.

PRAY WHAT YOU GOT

Like us, you may also struggle with knowing exactly *what* to say or *how* to pray. Sure, we can memorize some corporate Christian prayers, such as the Lord's Prayer (Matthew 6:9–13), but it's still entirely possible to pray "the right way" with nothing more than hollow religious words and a disengaged heart. And if that's the case, we are praying the *wrong* way.

I'd love to alleviate some of that pressure and weariness with something I heard Matt Chandler teach on the topic: "Just pray what you got." God doesn't want us to slap on a smile and say "spiritual" things we don't really mean. He doesn't ask us to use rigid religious language in order to approach him. More than anything, our Father God desires a genuine relationship with each one of us. He literally designed and created us to know him and to enjoy him.

We shouldn't pray to God because we are supposed to. We should pray because we are invited to. Through Jesus, you and I have access to personally engage with the creator of the heavens and the earth at any moment on any day. Whether it's good or bad, happy or hard, reflections or questions, gratitude or grumbling, just "pray what you got." As you do, over time, don't be surprised when you begin to approach your Heavenly Father more confidently, comfortably, and consistently. And don't be surprised if you begin to know him more, even if you understand him less.

1. **How would you each assess your prayer life at this time?** Do you feel like it is connected and thriving, or distant and stagnant?

2. **Discuss how you each have viewed the purpose of prayer.** How has that view helped or hindered your prayer life up to this point?

3. **Can you look back and name a time that God has answered a prayer differently than you asked, and it still amazed you?** Share these stories together to build your faith in God's wisdom, timing, and kindness.

4. **Today, which of your prayers are you most frustrated that God has not "answered" in the way you've asked, hoped, or expected?** Have you considered that God may be answering differently than you are asking? What emotions does that evoke?

5. **Do either of you feel the pressure to "pray the right way" instead of simply connecting openly with God?** If so, how can you commit to "praying what you got" and bringing your vulnerable prayers to him?

GUIDED PRAYER

Today, we're going to make it as basic as we discussed.

Take a moment to skim the discussion questions and scriptures above. Call to mind what you've just processed. Then, whether it's thirty seconds or thirty minutes, simply "pray what you got." There is no wrong way to start and no wrong way to wrap up.

If you have a hard time getting started, try simply finishing these thoughts:

God, I feel . . .

God, I wish . . .

God, I'm struggling with . . .

God, help me to . . .

He's listening. Pray what you got.

WHY ME?

"The temptation to compare is as near as your next chat with a friend, trip to the store, or check in on social media. And whether you come out on top or come up lacking, there is simply no win in comparison. It's a trap."
—Andy Stanley, *The Comparison Trap* video series

DANIEL

There's a popular saying from Theodore Roosevelt that goes, "Comparison is the thief of joy." It's true that one of the quickest paths to discontentment is to look longingly at what other people are experiencing, the good things they get to enjoy that we don't, or the hard things we have to navigate that they don't. It's okay to honestly acknowledge that it can be painful to watch others receive what you long for while you exist without it. It sucks, and we are allowed to say so. As we wrestle with God, we will likely wrestle with comparison as well.

THE COMPARISON TRAP

This question in its many forms can hit us when we take a look around, and it seems like we are carrying a disproportionate load of hardship compared to others. *"How come so many painful things seem to be happening to me and only me? Why does that person seem to have it so easy? Why does this person get to enjoy that blessing while we are left waiting and wanting?"*

SCRIPTURE

"Humble yourselves, therefore, under God's mighty hand, that he may lift you up in due time. Cast all your anxiety on him because he cares for you." —1 Peter 5:6–7

"A heart at peace gives life to the body, but envy rots the bones." —Proverbs 14:30

It all just feels unjust and unfair, and it becomes difficult not to get caught in the comparison trap.

While our third week will be entirely devoted to relational dynamics amid suffering, I'll go ahead and venture to guess that you have had a difficult time with certain people in your life during this season of sadness and sorrow. Furthermore, you may be finding that it can feel increasingly difficult to celebrate others around you and increasingly easy to resent them instead. You probably feel bad and even ashamed of these emotions, but they are real.

- *It's hard* watching other marriages thrive while yours struggles, or losing your spouse while other couples grow older and more deeply in love.

- *It's hard* praying desperately and diligently for your teen's struggle with a disorder or an addiction while other parents fret about grades and sports.

- *It's hard* seeing other parents take their children's perfect health for granted as you go from appointment to appointment or treatment after treatment.

- *It's hard* watching your peers live comfortably and confidently while you're navigating job loss and fighting to scrape by.

- *It's hard* to watch friends get pregnant effortlessly (or even accidentally) while you face disappointment month after month after month.

- *It's hard* suffering multiple miscarriages, and it's even harder as other moms deliver healthy baby after healthy baby.

- *It's hard* to watch those children hit milestones that yours never will.

- *It's hard* watching a parent or mentor begin to forget who you are, while other grandparents remain actively and joyfully engaged.

- It's all just *really, really hard.*

The battle with comparison can be compounded when it feels like others are enjoying success and blessings they haven't deserved or even sought out for themselves. The biblical authors consistently struggled with the undeniable observation that so many godless people and institutions seem to prosper while so many godly people seem to suffer. When the wicked flourish and the faithful flounder, it feels . . . backward.

WHAT BEGAN AS A BATTLE WITH COMPARISON LEADS TO A BATTLE FOR CONTROL.

GRASPING FOR CONTROL

As I have said, those sentiments are natural and normal. However, if we can't get a grip on the comparison game growing in our hearts, we'll find that it can become much more than a thief of our joy. Soon enough, we will find ourselves on a subtle and slippery slope that will lead us to doubt God's wisdom. Are we sure he knows what he's doing? Is he even paying attention? What began as a battle with comparison leads to a battle for control. Initially, we just decide to help God out a bit and make sure he gets this one right. But eventually, we find ourselves replacing him completely.

This is at the very heart of the enemy's strategy, and we see it all the way back in the earliest human temptation at the scene of the Fall. At the very beginning of our Bibles, in Genesis 3:1–7, the serpent slithered up to the first humans with a shrewd plan: not to pitch a blatant mutiny against God, but to plant seeds of doubt against God. *"Why would he not want you to eat from the best tree? Do you think he might be holding out on you, or holding you back? I mean, are you even sure that God can be trusted?"* It's sneaky and it's subtle. It's evil and it's effective. And for thousands of years, every one of their human descendants has been buying the same lie: God is ripping you off, and if you truly want your best life now, you need to make it happen *for yourself.*

"The original lies of the enemy were these: God isn't good, his word isn't true, and disobeying him is not that big of a deal."
—Todd Wagner, *Come and See*

FREEDOM IN SURRENDER

If you are on the hunt for an approach to life that will lead to anxiety, fear, mistrust, and manipulation, then just take the serpent at his word. Consider what you don't have and grasp for what you desire. But if you are seeking mental and emotional freedom, then, ironically, that will only be found in surrender by giving up control and placing matters entirely into God's hands. The choice is entirely yours, so please don't miss this. If you get nothing else from this day, we hope you will allow this truth to sink in. Full surrender to the Lord is where lasting peace, joy, and freedom are found. When our flesh tells us to compare our circumstances to those around us, may the Spirit help us look to God's heart and trust in his wisdom. He doesn't want to rip us off, he wants to set us free.

BUT IF YOU ARE SEEKING MENTAL AND EMOTIONAL FREEDOM, THEN, IRONICALLY, THAT WILL ONLY BE FOUND IN SURRENDER BY GIVING UP CONTROL AND PLACING MATTERS ENTIRELY INTO GOD'S HANDS.

1. **In what ways might you be struggling with comparison or control?** Do you feel resentful when people seem to have it "easier" or "better" than you? Do you typically desire to find solutions and strive to fix things? Do you become frustrated when you are powerless to change your circumstances?

2. **In what ways can you help each other fight the desire to compare and control?** What are specific areas that consistently foster discontentment? Would it be helpful to consider limiting or removing access to those things that steal your joy?

3. **Is it difficult for you to take God at his word?** In what ways is it tempting to believe that he is holding out on you? How do you think comparison and control might be playing into these temptations?

4. **What about surrendering control to God elicits the most fear?** What is the #1 thing holding you back?

5. **Lastly, what are 2–3 things that you are truly grateful for?** Despite life's struggles and imperfections, what are some of the biggest blessings God has given you? Share these with each other.

1. **We're going to invite you to take a bold step.** It's an invitation to let go and lay it all down. If you'd like to do so, take a moment and take a deep breath. Ask God to help you surrender the desire to control your life and compare your life to others. Commit to praying for one another in this way and check in with one another in the coming days.

2. **Take a moment to stop and thank God for the many blessings in your life,** including the things you said you were most grateful for above. Few things will attune your hearts in a posture of prayer like the practice of gratitude.

3. **Personalize and pray the following,** and feel encouraged to add anything else that you'd like to tell God. If you feel comfortable doing so, you could hold hands and do this together.

God, we confess that most days, we don't trust you like we want to.

We confess that we want to control our own lives rather than entrust them to you.

Despite your many blessings, we are tempted to believe you're holding out on us.

We are tempted to look at our surroundings rather than our Savior.

Help us see the beauty in our stories, rather than wishing for another one.

Help us remember and reflect upon your abundant faithfulness to us.

Help us to let go and lay our burdens at your feet, for your glory and our good.

One day at a time.

Amen.

WILL THIS EVER END?

SCRIPTURE

"And I heard a loud voice from the throne saying, 'Look! God's dwelling place is now among the people, and he will dwell with them. They will be his people, and God himself will be with them and be their God. He will wipe every tear from their eyes. There will be no more death or mourning or crying or pain, for the old order of things has passed away.' He who was seated on the throne said, 'I am making everything new!' Then he said, 'Write this down, for these words are trustworthy and true.'"
—Revelation 21:3–5

Yesterday, we briefly mentioned one temptation in a garden, and today we'll start with another. The most significant moment of wrestling with God in the entire Bible occurred in the middle of the night in the moonlit garden of Gethsemane, where the earthly life and ministry of Jesus came to its climax: the final and greatest test (Matthew 26:36–56). Just imagine the mental, emotional, and spiritual agony that Jesus must have felt as he awaited his captors. The thoughts running through his mind. The war raging in his heart. The terrible fear of knowing what laid ahead for him if he didn't run. Hearing voices get louder and seeing torches getting closer and closer.

We'll conclude a heavy first week with an honest question in those garden-like moments of anguish and despair. *"Will this sorrow and suffering ever come to pass?"* Or as Jesus prayed on that agonizing night, *"My father, if it is possible, may this cup be taken from me?"* (Matthew 26:39). There are two truthful but different responses for us. If we are primarily looking at our human experience and asking if things will ever change, we simply do not and cannot know that. Whatever you're walking through may last for a season or a lifetime. However, if we are looking beyond our earthly lives toward eternity, God's response became crystal clear about two thousand years ago.

IN A WEEK FULL OF DAUNTING QUESTION MARKS,
I WANT TO FINISH WITH GOD'S DEFINITIVE
EXCLAMATION POINT, THE CRUCIFIXION AND
RESURRECTION OF JESUS.

THE GOOD NEWS OF THE GOSPEL

I want to lay out the single most important truth you'll read in this or any book. I'm going to unpack the explicit gospel (or "good news") of Jesus Christ and what he came to accomplish on our behalf. In a week full of daunting question marks, I want to finish with God's definitive exclamation point, the crucifixion and resurrection of Jesus. In doing so, we will zero in on our ultimate (and only) source of unceasing hope. Whenever we find ourselves downward spiraling in sorrow, the single best thing we can do is look back at the life, death, and resurrection of God's son. He has gone to no uncertain lengths to communicate how he feels about you, and how far he was willing to go in order to win us back to himself. This salvation came at a terrible cost to him so that it might now be offered freely to us.

As always, the word of God says it better than I ever could, so I'll let it speak for itself. In his letter to the church in Ephesus, the apostle Paul lays out the gospel message. You'll see that it begins with some sobering bad news, but that's what makes the rest of the "good news" so very good, indeed.

As for you, you were dead in your transgressions and sins, in which you used to live when you followed the ways of this world and of the ruler of the kingdom of the air, the spirit who is now at work in those who are disobedient. All of us also lived among them at one time, gratifying the cravings of our flesh and following its desires and thoughts. Like the rest, we were by nature deserving of wrath.

But because of his great love for us, God, who is rich in mercy, made us alive with Christ even when we were dead in transgressions—it is by grace you have been saved. And God raised us up with Christ and seated us with him in the heavenly realms in Christ Jesus, in order that in the coming ages he might show the incomparable riches of his grace, expressed in his kindness to us in Christ Jesus. For it is by grace you have been saved, through faith—and this is not from yourselves, it is the gift of God—not by works, so that no one can boast. For we are God's handiwork, created in Christ Jesus to do good works, which God prepared in advance for us to do (Ephesians 2:1–10).

Apart from the Lord intervening on our behalf, we are helpless and we are hopeless in this fallen world. And yet, because of his great love for his children, God has bridged the gap with a wooden cross. He doesn't take bad people and make them good; that is not Christianity. Heaven will not be full of "good" people; it will be full of *forgiven* people who have been pulled out of spiritual death and brought into spiritual life. That is the gospel, and that is the unshakable source of our living hope, now and forevermore.

NOT OUR FOREVER HOME

In the meantime, Jesus was pretty straightforward when he told his disciples, "In this world, you will have trouble." He didn't say we could, or we might—he said *we will have trouble* in this broken world. Following Jesus does not exempt us from pain and sorrow. Thankfully there's a second half to that statement, and in the face of certain suffering, Jesus exhorts his followers, "But take heart! I have overcome the world" (John 16:33).

Jesus' triumphant victory over sin and death may not alleviate our undesirable situations in the here and now, but it transforms everything about our "not yet." This world as we know it is not our home, and our Father will one day bring about a new creation on earth as it is in heaven. All that is broken will be restored. All that is wrong will be made right. And not one ounce of our pain will have been wasted. Until that time comes, our humble prayer in the coming weeks is that you might invite him to make you a new creation, perhaps for the very first time.

> Therefore, if anyone is in Christ, the new creation has come: the old has gone, the new is here! All this is from God, who reconciled us to himself through Christ and gave us the ministry of reconciliation: that God was reconciling the world to himself in Christ, not counting people's sins against them. And he has committed to us the message of reconciliation (2 Corinthians 5:17–19).

No matter who you are, the date on your calendar hinges and pivots around the coming of Jesus two thousand years ago. The same is true of our souls. He is the fork in the road of this life that determines our destination in the life to come, and there are only two options. This world and this life will either be your heaven or your hell. Apart from Jesus, this is as good as it will get. What a grim, troubling thought. But *through* Jesus, these years are the closest thing to hell we will ever know. Take heart, for he has overcome it.

"Life with God is not immunity from difficulties, but peace in difficulties." —Arthur James Russell

1. **Have either of you felt at the breaking point of despair?** When have you felt the most hopeless? What emotions are you tired of feeling?

2. **Even if you've had exposure to the Bible or to church,** did anything about the message of Christianity pop in a new way today? How so?

3. **How has the Gospel message impacted your perspective on your current sufferings?** What stood out the most to you as you read Ephesians 2:1–10?

4. **Have you personally trusted in the good news of the Gospel?** If not, what is holding you back?

1. **Go back and reread Ephesians 2:1–10 out loud with one another.** Take a moment to meditate on the weight of the "bad news" in verses 1–3, and the "good news" in verses 4–10.

2. **If you've never personally processed, identified with, and accepted those truths for yourself,** we want to give you that opportunity. Even if you have, we still invite you to close this first week by repeating and reveling in the single most important message the world has ever known.

God, I know that I am a sinner, spiritually dead in my transgressions.

We live in a fallen world, and my personal sin contributes to that brokenness.

I deserve the consequences of my sin, which is eternal separation from you.

I recognize that I am helpless, hopeless, and powerless to change or save myself.

However,

I believe that Jesus has made a way through his death and resurrection.

I believe that eternal life is not something I earn but receive as a free gift in him.

I trust in Jesus, and Jesus alone, as my Savior from sin and the Lord of my life.

I will not be perfect, but I will follow Jesus and joyfully come under his authority.

Like him, I know I will suffer in this life. But through him, a glorious future awaits.

Thank you, God, for saving me and forgiving me!

Amen.

WEEK TWO

MYTHS & TRUTHS

"

"But each and every time, when our 'wisdom' is employed in place of God's sovereign and mysterious ways, it has not gone well."

Before we packed up for our stint in Haiti, we were given some recommended reading to learn a guiding framework for how to alleviate poverty strategically and biblically. The book is called *When Helping Hurts*.

WHEN HELPING HURTS

The basic premise is that it is entirely possible to have the best of intentions in coming alongside someone, but unknowingly make matters worse rather than better. Instead of empowering someone, we may be enabling them. There are actions that may look like solutions but ultimately fail to alter one's trajectory toward lasting health and healing. There are methods that may provide temporary relief on the surface but leave the deepest needs unaddressed and unresolved. You get the idea.

I think this same notion can be applied more broadly to many of our most common efforts to comfort and console people who are in a place of emotional and spiritual anguish. More specifically, and sadly, we are seeing many of the world's prominent Christian churches and leaders put forth doctrines and teachings that are not simply unbiblical and unhelpful; they are leading people to a place of desperation, destruction, and despair. At worst, these voices and their counsel are intentionally manipulative and evil to the core. At best, there are thousands of shepherds who genuinely believe they are helping, but they are actually *hurting* the sheep.

While it doesn't make it less discouraging to watch, it's important to know that this is not a new phenomenon. We see it in the Gospel accounts as Jesus confronted the corrupt religious establishment of his day. We certainly see it in Paul's New Testament letters, as he repeatedly warns his disciples about the dangers of false teachers in and out of the church. And indeed, we see it way back in early Old Testament times.

A MAN NAMED JOB

Placed near the middle of your Bible, there is an entire book that zooms in on one man's honest wrestling with God in the midst of unthinkable afflictions. The book is called Job, which is actually this man's name, not his employment status (bad dad joke). Many scholars believe that chronically, Job was recorded in the times of Genesis and thus one the earliest pieces of Scripture we have.

Largely poetic, just like the psalms, the book of Job is actually classified as "wisdom literature." Here, before the coming of Christ and before God's covenants with Abraham or David, we are given an extremely valuable and relevant revelation on the topic of human suffering. Forgive the spoilers if you haven't read his story, but in the earliest chapters we watch Job suddenly and tragically lose his children, his resources, and his health. Let me say that again, more slowly.

Job's sons and daughters are all senselessly killed.

Job's sources of financial security and material provision are taken away.

Job's physical body becomes hard to look at and harder to live in.

Children. Wealth. Health. Gone.

In this place of unfathomable loss and pain, a few of Job's friends come to comfort him. At first, they simply sit with him in his grief and say nothing. Unfortunately, their silence ends up being the best thing he gets from them. Once they open their mouths, they feel the need to try and reason with Job about why he is suffering, making plenty of assertions and assumptions about Job and about God. Pretty soon, any notion of "comfort" goes out the window. In his words, "You are miserable comforters, all of you!" (Job 16:2).

BAD ANSWERS TO GOOD QUESTIONS

Just as Job's story has lived on, I'm afraid the approach of Job's "friends" has lived on as well. There have *always* been man-made attempts to answer the unanswerable. In our desire to resolve some of the weighty questions we walked through last week, humans have cooked up countless philosophies and explanations for when life doesn't go the way we hoped or expected. But each and every time, when our "wisdom" is employed in place of God's sovereign and mysterious ways, it has not gone well.

In short, we have seen really bad theology throughout all of biblical history, and indeed, throughout all of *human* history. Last week, we wrestled with many of the same questions and objections that Job was surely thinking and feeling. This week, we will explore a handful of the ways that human thinkers have sought to explain the causes of our sufferings and alleviate the agony of the unresolved. Said another way, we will dissect some of the ways that our honest, fair, and good questions have been met with some really *bad* answers, and correct these cultural myths with biblical truths.

HEALTHY, WEALTHY, AND BLESSED?

If you're on social media, you've surely seen #blessed at the end of a post containing photographs of people enjoying good fortune and "the good life." While the Scriptures show repeatedly that God desires to bless his people, what has become warped and convoluted over time is exactly what it means to be "blessed."

Cultural myth: God always blesses his people with physical, worldly prosperity.

Biblical truth: God always blesses his people with spiritual, heavenly prosperity.

SCRIPTURE

"Whoever gives thought to the word will discover good, and blessed is he who trusts in the Lord." —Proverbs 16:20

"Praise be to the God and Father of our Lord Jesus Christ, who has blessed us in the heavenly realms with every spiritual blessing in Christ." —Ephesians 1:3

PROSPERITY THEOLOGY

Last week, we talked about how what comes to our mind when we think about God is the single most important thing about us. If we may be so bold as to extend that thought, we would add the following: what comes to our mind when we think about being "blessed" will significantly impact our view of God. For that reason, few heresies have plagued the Church like the "prosperity gospel": the belief that God rewards the righteous with increases in health and wealth. It teaches that if humans have faith in God, he will surely shower us with security and success. Sadly, this theology originated right here in the land of the American Dream, spreading with the rise of "televangelists" such as Benny Hinn. Nowadays, names likely to ring a bell include pastors like Joel Osteen, author of titles such as *Your Best Life Now, It's Your Time, and You Can, You Will.*

It begs the question, Where do prosperity preachers get this idea? Much is derived from nontraditional interpretations or misapplications of specific Bible verses. As an example of how this slippery slope might look, you may recognize Jeremiah 29:11, which says, "'For I know the plans I have for you,' declares the Lord, 'plans to *prosper* you and not to harm you, plans to give you hope and a future'" (emphasis added).

For starters, when read in context, we will see that this specific promise was given to the Israelite captives who were exiled to Babylon in the sixth century BC. God is reaffirming his commitment to bring them back into the promised land, and fulfilled his word in 539 BC. Does God have plans and purposes that can be trusted today? Absolutely, but it would be a mistake to interpret that his plan is to "prosper" all Christians based on Jeremiah 29. Furthermore, it would be a mistake to conclude that God intends to "prosper" us in the worldly sense of the word.

BLESSED, BIBLICALLY

Even outside of the prosperity gospel, the way many Christians have come to define (or should I say redefine) the idea of being "blessed" is very different from the biblical authors. Thankfully, a holistic look at God's Word can help us set the record straight. First and fundamentally, while God certainly blesses the righteous, that blessing does not always (or even usually) take material form. If it did, we would have no way to explain the anguish and deprivation

FIRST AND FUNDAMENTALLY, WHILE GOD CERTAINLY BLESSES THE RIGHTEOUS, THAT BLESSING DOES NOT ALWAYS (OR EVEN USUALLY) TAKE MATERIAL FORM.

suffered by the apostles, martyrs, or faithful Christians around the world (Hebrews 11:35–40).

Simply look at the life and *lifestyle* of Jesus himself. Rather than emphasizing comfort and material prosperity, he repeatedly warns us about the dangers of pursuing those things. Jesus' most famous message, the Sermon on the Mount, actually begins by defining who is truly blessed (Matthew 5:3–12). As you read his list of blessings, you'll find that Jesus doesn't mention one thing about physical or external circumstances. Well, I take that back, he does tell them they will likely be persecuted for our faith. So much for health and wealth!

GotQuestions.org is an incredible resource that skillfully summarizes the Scriptures, and it provides the following overview of these opening words from Jesus:

> Jesus used the term *blessed* to describe the inner quality of a faithful servant of God. This blessedness is a spiritual state of well-being—a

deep, joy-filled contentment that cannot be shaken by poverty, grief, famine, persecution, war, or any other trial or tragedy we face in life. In human terms, the situations he describes are far from blessings. But because God is present with us through these difficult times, we are actually blessed by him in them.

Simply put, we are trained to feel blessed when we get what we want. We don't want to suffer, so the idea of being blessed in the midst of suffering is hard for us to wrap our minds around. But as we define blessing biblically, we begin to see that because of Christ's sufferings on the cross, we are blessed even in the midst of ours. His blessing is not a future hypothetical but a present reality for every believer.

THE PATH TO TRUE PROSPERITY

We would love to close with the way that the book of Psalms actually opens. "Blessed is the one who does not walk in step with the wicked or stand in the way that sinners take or sit in the company of mockers, but whose delight is in the law of the Lord, and who meditates on his law day and night. That person is like a tree planted by streams of water, which yields its fruit in season and whose leaf does not wither—whatever they do *prospers*" (Psalm 1:1–3, emphasis added).

May we pursue God rather than the pleasures of this world. May we dwell on his Word, delight in his ways, and deepen our roots in him. May we realize that being truly, biblically blessed speaks to our *spiritual* prosperity rather than our physical prosperity, and may we discover a joy that is stronger than our sorrows. God is calling us to seek him in seasons of suffering, and we will find that we can be faithful and fruitful. This is the path to true biblical prosperity. It may leave us hurting, but it will *never* leave us wanting.

1. **Up to this point, consider how you have viewed and defined what it means to be "blessed" by God.** Is your answer closer to the world's definition or the Bible's definition? Where did each of you develop this worldview?

2. **How has that view of the "blessed" life affected your view of the suffering you have experienced?** Has it helped or hindered your walk with God?

3. **Do you find yourself desiring physical and material prosperity more than spiritual prosperity?** If so, you're not the only one, but how can you reshape your perspective to experience God's blessing in all circumstances? What scriptures could you memorize, and what reminders do you each need?

4. **Have you seen any spiritual blessings come from this season of hardship?** There is no pressure to discover any just yet, but we'd love for you to consider this question in the coming weeks and months.

5. **Do the biblical definitions of blessing and prosperity help you see your suffering in a different light?** Why or why not?

1. **Take a moment to acknowledge** and articulate to God the ways that you often desire "worldly" blessings and prosperity before spiritual blessings and prosperity.

2. **If you can do so genuinely, invite God to help you see the spiritual blessings available to you even in this difficult time.** If you're not there yet, pray that the days and weeks ahead will help move you closer to that and closer to him.

3. **Personalize and pray the following,** and feel encouraged to add anything else that you'd like to tell God. If you feel comfortable doing so, you could hold hands and do this together.

God, you alone are the source of true blessing and prosperity.

You are better than anything this world has to offer.

Thank you for your kindness and nearness even in the midst of my pain.

Help me see the blessings in my life, by your standards and not the world's.

Help me delight in you and enjoy a life that is faithful and fruitful in every season.

One day at a time.

Amen.

CAN I HAVE ENOUGH FAITH?

SCRIPTURE

"Now faith is confidence in what we hope for and assurance about what we do not see." —Hebrews 11:1

"If we are thrown into the blazing furnace, the God we serve is able to deliver us from it, and he will deliver us from Your Majesty's hand. But even if he does not, we want you to know, Your Majesty, that we will not serve your gods or worship the image of gold you have set up." —Daniel 3:17–18

Following Abel's life-limiting diagnosis, we believed we could trust God and rest in his sovereignty while loving Abel every day we were given. But it also occurred to us that Jesus tells his followers to ask, seek, and knock (Matthew 7:7). While trusting *his* heart, he invites us to ask him for whatever is heavy on *our* hearts. Of course we wanted our son to be healed and be here with us for years and decades to come. So that's what we began to do. In faith, we asked God to heal Abel's body.

Cultural myth: If I have enough faith, then God will change my circumstances.

Biblical truth: I can have peace in all circumstances because Christ is enough.

THE "WORD OF FAITH" MOVEMENT

Another prevalent outgrowth of prosperity theology has come to be known as the "word of faith" movement. In *God, Greed, and the (Prosperity) Gospel*, Costi Hinn summarizes this belief as one that "demeans God to the position of a puppet and elevates man to the position of a puppet master who makes confessional demands by faith.

It does this by considering faith as a force and God as the one who must respond to our faith. This is a heretical twisting of true faith." A heretical twisting, indeed, as "faith" becomes more like a magic wand in our pocket than a submissive trust in God's will and way. It makes God predictable and controllable, and it obligates him to bring about whatever we are asking for. He's no longer a person we engage with but a formula we manipulate.

IT DOES THIS BY CONSIDERING FAITH AS A FORCE AND GOD AS THE ONE WHO MUST RESPOND TO OUR FAITH.

At the very beginning of this workbook, I shared Elisabeth Elliot's broad and simplified definition for suffering: *having what you don't want, or wanting what you don't have.* If we build off that basic sentiment, what do you think happens when our suffering intersects with "word of faith" teachings? Satisfaction will elude you; you cannot fathom sustained suffering as a believer. Without a change in circumstance, you will be without contentment. Needless to say, this is not the life God intends for his beloved children, and this is a false representation of what Christianity and the Bible teaches.

WHATEVER THE CIRCUMSTANCES

As a picture of the subtle shift from biblical faith to "word of faith" theology, I think about another common misapplication of the popular Bible verse, "I can do all things through him who gives me strength" (Philippians 4:13). I see how someone might interpret that isolated statement to mean, "With a little help from God, I can achieve anything and gain everything." But in that arrangement, it's ultimately not God that I want, but the success he can bring if I have "faith"—and before we know it, we've departed from true gospel faith and arrived back at the prosperity gospel. So in the spirit of reading Scripture in its context, let's include the two verses prior to capture what Paul is actually saying here:

> I am not saying this because I am in need, for I have learned to *be content whatever the circumstances.* I know what it is to be in need, and I know what it is to have plenty. I have learned the secret of being content in any and every situation, whether well fed or hungry, *whether living in plenty or in want.* I can do all this through him who gives me strength (Philippians 4:11–13, emphasis added).

You see, Paul is not saying that Christians will gain what we desire and accomplish whatever we set our minds to. His point is precisely the opposite as he writes these words from a prison cell, not a penthouse. He's telling us that life will *not* always go the way we desire, and we *will* be left wanting. There will be seasons of deep satisfaction, seasons of deep suffering, and everything in between. True faith is trusting that we can face anything life throws our way, knowing that he is with us, he is for us, and he is enough for us in each and every circumstance. Paul is saying, "Jesus will sustain me on my darkest days, and I can be okay in all circumstances because he is all I need." As he writes earlier in the very same chapter, "And the peace of God, which transcends all understanding, will guard your hearts and your minds in Christ Jesus" (Philippians 4:7).

1:29 P.M.

Around the same time we felt led to pray for Abel's physical healing, a sweet friend asked if she could set an alarm on her phone to remind her to pray for us and for Abel every day. We went with 1:29 p.m., his original due date, and loved the idea so much that we decided to loop in all of our friends and family. We also shared about it on the blog we had been keeping, which ended up being viewed over a quarter of a million times in the months that followed. Literally hundreds of phones were going off every single day across the country and the world, prompting people to talk to their Father about our son. We are sharing this because we want to show you that Abel may have been one of the most prayed for babies of all time ... and yet, his condition was not healed. Our son was born with Trisomy 18 and we said goodbye fifteen days later.

Did all of those prayers "not work"? Did we not pull the right levers? Did we simply not have enough faith? You can see what a wretched burden this would place on those who embrace a "word of faith" theology. No, those 1:29 p.m. prayers didn't change the outcome of Abel's story—but they did do something miraculous. They changed us and changed others. And though God didn't extend Abel's earthly life, he did heal his body, in the fullest and ultimate sense.

In faith, we didn't run from God—we ran to him. In faith, we didn't make demands of God—we made a point to trust him. In faith, we knew that God could heal our son—we knew that he might not. "And by faith, Abel still speaks, even though he is dead" (Hebrews 11:4b). We can have peace in all circumstances because Christ is enough.

"Then Jesus went with his disciples to a place called Gethsemane, and he said to them, 'Sit here while I go over there and pray.' He took Peter and the two sons of Zebedee along with him, and he began to be sorrowful and troubled. Then he said to them, 'My soul is overwhelmed with sorrow to the point of death. Stay here and keep watch with me.' Going a little farther, he fell with his face to the ground and prayed, 'My Father, if it is possible, may this cup be taken from me. Yet not as I will, but as you will.'" —Matthew 26:36–39

TRUE FAITH IS TRUSTING THAT WE CAN FACE ANYTHING LIFE THROWS OUR WAY, KNOWING THAT HE IS WITH US, HE IS FOR US, AND HE IS ENOUGH FOR US IN EACH AND EVERY CIRCUMSTANCE.

1. **Do either of you find yourselves believing that God would change your circumstances if you just had enough faith?** Where do you think that came from?

2. **Have you ever felt called to pray for something specific and then didn't get the answer you were hoping for?** How did that make you feel, and what conclusions did you draw?

3. **Do you both believe that even when you don't get the answer you longed for, that Jesus is still enough for you?** And do you believe that even in suffering, you can have peace in all circumstances?

4. **How can you commit to helping each other reject false teachings and believe the true Gospel?** What could it look like to continually point each other back to the truth in the midst of your heartache?

1. **Take a moment to acknowledge** and articulate to God if you've ever viewed your faith as a means to coerce or control him.

2. **If you can do so genuinely, pray that courageous prayer of Christ in the garden of Gethsemane:** "My Father, if it is possible, may this cup be taken from me. Yet not as I will, but as you will." If you're not there yet, pray that the days and weeks ahead will help move you closer to that and closer to him.

3. **Personalize and pray the following,** and feel encouraged to add anything else that you'd like to tell God. If you feel comfortable doing so, you could hold hands and do this together.

God, you are a good God and you owe us absolutely nothing.

Thank you for inviting my honest prayers and hearing every one of them.

I confess that it is hard to find contentment in this season of suffering.

Help me experience your peace that surpasses understanding.

Help me to have confidence in you in each and every circumstance.

One day at a time.

Amen.

WHAT GOES AROUND COMES AROUND?

SCRIPTURE

"And the Lord said to Satan, 'Have you considered my servant Job, that there is none like him on the earth, a blameless and upright man, who fears God and turns away from evil?'" Then Satan answered the Lord and said . . . "You have blessed the work of his hands, so that his flocks and herds are spread throughout the land. But stretch out your hand and strike all that he has, and he will surely curse you to your face." —Job 1:8, 10–11

"And Job said, 'Naked I came from my mother's womb, and naked shall I return. The Lord gave, and the Lord has taken away; blessed be the name of the Lord.'" —Job 1:21

"Though he slay me, I will hope in him; yet I will argue my ways to his face." —Job 13:15

DANIEL

I am incredibly grateful to have a car, but taking it to the shop for repairs is never fun. One time, I forgot to change my oil . . . for two years. That didn't go well for the ol' Crawford-mobile, and it was directly and entirely my fault. Another time, my window got shattered by someone breaking into it. That one was all their doing, but I'm the one who paid for it. Yet another time, a piece of someone's shredded tire flew up and put a massive dent in my front bumper. I didn't feel like I "deserved" that either, but it's hard to blame anyone there. I was just at the wrong place at the wrong time. In the same way, the damage and hardship in our lives can sometimes be traced back to specific actions or decisions, but not always. Sometimes, we just catch the brunt of living in a fallen world.

Cultural myth: Our suffering is always because God is punishing us for something.

Biblical truth: Our suffering is not always associated with our sin.

THESE "MISERABLE COMFORTERS" (JOB 16:2) ARE MUCH
LIKE THE PROSPERITY PREACHERS WHO ASSUME THAT GOD
REWARDS THE RIGHTEOUS IF THEY BELIEVE HARD ENOUGH,
WHILE THOSE WITH WEAKER FAITH OR SECRET SIN WILL
REAP CALAMITIES.

JOB'S "FRIENDS"

As a refresher from this week's introduction, Job was a righteous man who was suddenly embroiled in an intense ordeal of suffering. As the reader, we get a peek behind the curtain in chapters 1–2 and see that these afflictions are not indicative of God's judgment on Job, but his confidence in Job. While he permits the suffering that ensues at the hands of the enemy, God does not ordain it. Job goes through three cycles of debates with his friends in chapters 3–39, who offer all sorts of possibilities for why Job was going through such suffering. These "miserable comforters" (Job 16:2) are much like the prosperity preachers who assume that God rewards the righteous if they believe hard enough, while those with weaker faith or secret sin will reap calamities.

Their assumption is that anyone who suffers is somehow "getting what they deserve." When we flip to the final epilogue, however, God condemns them for the lousy counsel. "I am angry with you and your two friends, *because you have not spoken the truth about me,* as my servant Job has'" (Job 42:7b,

emphasis added). It's clear that these men got it wrong, so let's see what we can learn from the one who always got it right.

WHAT WOULD JESUS SAY?

In Jesus' own day, we see the same flawed assumption made by his own disciples. "As he went along, Jesus saw a man blind from birth. His disciples asked him, 'Rabbi, who sinned, this man or his parents, that he was born blind?' Jesus said, 'Neither this man nor his parents sinned, but this happened so that the works of God might be displayed in him'" (John 9:1–3).

In their minds, it wasn't *if* someone had sinned but *who* had sinned in this family. But Jesus says that this man's affliction was not anyone's "fault" and it was not a result of God's judgment. On the contrary, it was about to become a cause for God's glory as this man's eyes opened, not only in the physical sense but in the spiritual sense. He was able to see who Jesus was, both as a man in the flesh and as the savior of the world (John 9:35–38).

"The difference between what Job knew of God in prosperity and what he knew of him through adversity was the difference between 'hearing and knowing' about God and truly experiencing God." —Bruce Wilkinson and Kenneth Boa, *Talk Thru the Bible*

Far from punishment, God can actually use our afflictions as part of His divine plan to strengthen our faith and transform our lives for His glory. Though many who do wrong will often suffer as a result, God also permits suffering for reasons entirely unknown to us. We should always examine our hearts and assess our lives before the Lord (Psalm 139:23–24), but we never assume that our suffering is judgment for sin.

KARMA VS. GRACE

According to the theory of karma, whatever you experience in this life is the inevitable result of actions (good or bad) in a previous life—an endless cycle of cause and effect, punishment and reward. This is one of the most fundamental ways that Christianity is different from Hinduism, Buddhism, and every other religious worldview. The God of the Bible is absolutely just—but he is also merciful and gracious.

Karma says, "Good or bad, you'll always get what you deserve."

Mercy says, "I'm *not* going to give you the bad consequence you do deserve."

Grace says, "I'm going to give you a good gift you *don't* deserve."

Last week, we walked through the message of the gospel as summarized in Ephesians 2:1–10. Today, I'd like to close with another passage of Scripture capturing the essence of the gospel. Pause after the first part and recognize that we all fit in that category. Then read the rest and praise our Father for being a God of grace, not karma.

At one time we too were foolish, disobedient, deceived, and enslaved by all kinds of passions and pleasures. We lived in malice and envy, being hated and hating one another. But when the kindness and love of God our Savior appeared, he saved us, not because of righteous things we had done, but because of his mercy. He saved us through the washing of rebirth and renewal by the Holy Spirit, whom he poured out on us generously through Jesus Christ our Savior, so that, having been justified by his grace, we might become heirs having the hope of eternal life (Titus 3:3–7).

1. **Are either of you tempted to believe that your suffering is punishment for something you did in the past?** What lies is that speaking to you? (Even if you are suffering from a bad decision, know that God wants to use this pain for your good and his glory).

2. **What kind of advice have your friends given you in the midst of your suffering?** What advice do you hope to heed and cling to? Which advice should you throw out?

3. **Do you believe that God can use your suffering to strengthen your faith or the faith of those around you?** Have you seen that happen in your journey so far?

4. **What lies are you tempted to believe about your suffering?** Are you ever tempted to think that God's favor is based on your good or bad performance? Speak of God's grace and mercy to one another.

1. **Take a moment to acknowledge** and articulate to God any ways you have felt wronged or embittered toward him, believing he was the source of your affliction.

2. **If you can do so genuinely, invite God to help you trust him even in the absence of answers.** If you're not there yet, pray that the days and weeks ahead will help move you closer to that and closer to him.

3. **Personalize and pray the following,** and feel encouraged to add anything else that you'd like to tell God. If you feel comfortable doing so, you could hold hands and do this together.

God, your mercy and grace toward me is incomprehensible.

Thank you that you don't repay me for my sin or give me what I "deserve."

Even so, I recognize that your mercy does not make me immune from sorrow.

Help me trust in your heart and rest in your sovereignty.

I give you my circumstances and my life to be used for your purposes.

One day at a time.

Amen.

SURELY, I CAN HANDLE THIS?

SCRIPTURE

"Come to me, all you who are weary and burdened, and I will give you rest. Take my yoke upon you and learn from me, for I am gentle and humble in heart, and you will find rest for your souls. For my yoke is easy and my burden is light."
—Matthew 11:28–30

"Humble yourselves, therefore, under God's mighty hand, that he may lift you up in due time. Cast all your anxiety on him because he cares for you." —1 Peter 5:6–7

"For we do not want you to be unaware, brothers, of the affliction we experienced in Asia. For we were so utterly burdened beyond our strength that we despaired of life itself. Indeed, we felt that we had received the sentence of death. But that was to make us rely not on ourselves but on God who raises the dead." —2 Corinthians 1:8–9 ESV

A friend of ours told us a story about his son playing Tetris for the first time without reading any directions or seeing it played first. At first glance, he appeared to be the most awful Tetris player in history, until it was discovered that he thought the objective was to pile up the blocks as quickly as possible to reach the top of the screen, like a little two-dimensional Tower of Babel (Genesis 11:1–9). It's a laughable illustration of how we can unknowingly play the game of life entirely wrong. Ironically, rather than building yourself up, the Bible tells us that the path to true strength and success is to be broken down. In the words of John the Baptist, "He must increase, but I must decrease" (John 3:30, ESV).

Cultural myth: God wouldn't give me more than I can handle.

Biblical truth: Apart from God we can do nothing, but when we are weak he is strong.

DESIGNED FOR DEPENDENCE

Particularly in the modern West, we live in a culture that measures strength and success in the form of self-reliance and self-sufficiency. We

IF WE DESIRE A FRUITFUL LIFE, IT TAKES A DAILY
DECLARATION OF DEPENDENCE, AND IT STARTS WITH
TRADING OUR "STRENGTH" FOR HIS.

celebrate this when we see it in others and in ourselves. A "declaration of independence" is at our foundation, after all, and the essence of the American Dream is that we can pull ourselves up by our bootstraps and overcome anything with enough hard work and grit. We don't like asking for help even when we need it, and relying on anybody else is often a source of shame. But as we'll find, the essence of Christianity couldn't be more different from these views of independence and strength.

> *"If dependence is the goal, then weakness is the advantage."*
> —Jonathan Pokluda

Seasons of sorrow and suffering have a way of forcing us to come face-to-face with our human limitations. For that reason, our pain can actually be a blessing in disguise. It is not fun to come to the end of ourselves, but that is precisely where we will discover some of the greatest truths about how we are designed to live in relationship to God. The Scriptures are clear that God has specifically and intentionally created us for dependence upon him. The key to human flourishing does not rest in our hands, but his.

I am the true vine, and my Father is the gardener. He cuts off every branch in me that bears no fruit, while every branch that does bear fruit he prunes so that it will be even more fruitful. You are already clean because of the word I have spoken to you. Remain in me, as I also remain in you. No branch can bear fruit by itself; it must remain in the vine. Neither can you bear fruit unless you remain in me. I am the vine; you are the branches. If you remain in me and I in you, you will bear much fruit; apart from me, you can do nothing (John 15:1–5).

Recognizing that we can produce nothing of lasting value apart from him will feel humbling, or even humiliating. It's a blow to our ego, but that's exactly what we sometimes need. If we are seeking to stay connected to the vine and reorient our hearts to rely on Jesus, we must consistently acknowledge and articulate our need for him. If we desire a fruitful life, it takes a daily declaration of dependence, and it starts with trading our "strength" for his.

STRENGTH IN WEAKNESS

The Bible is clear that we are designed for godly dependence, and it is also clear that true strength is found in our God, not ourselves. The apostle Paul addresses this throughout his second letter to the Corinthian church, and one passage toward the end summarizes this truth beautifully:

> Therefore, in order to keep me from becoming conceited, I was given a thorn in my flesh, a messenger of Satan, to torment me. Three times I pleaded with the Lord to take it away from me. But he said to me, "My grace is sufficient for you, *for my power is made perfect in weakness."* Therefore I will boast all the more gladly about my weaknesses, so that Christ's power may rest on me. That is why, for Christ's sake, I delight in weaknesses, in insults, in hardships, in persecutions, in difficulties. *For when I am weak, then I am strong* (2 Corinthians 12:7b–10, emphasis added).

Whatever Paul's "thorn in the flesh" may have been, it served as an ever-present reminder of his own weakness and dependence upon the Lord. Paul was such a faithful and fruitful minister of the gospel— not in spite of his human frailty, but because of it. If I choose to operate out of my own strength, that is a losing strategy in this life. Paul figured out how to "play the game" the right way, and God worked in him and used him beyond his wildest imaginations.

The truth is that God will often give us more than we can handle on our own. Life will burden us with a weight that we simply cannot carry. He doesn't enjoy watching us struggle, but he loves us enough to let us come to the end of ourselves.

That may be right where you are, and if so, these words you're reading today are written just for you. God can handle what you are going through. All of this presents us with an incredibly liberating offer. We don't have to pretend or perform. Rather than feeling insecure about our shortcomings, we can revel in them because they lead us back to him. Declare your dependence and lay down your burdens. Find rest for your soul in a God whose power is made perfect in weakness. As we decrease, he will increase. Apart from God we can do nothing, but when we are weak he is strong.

HE DOESN'T ENJOY WATCHING US STRUGGLE, BUT HE LOVES US ENOUGH TO LET US COME TO THE END OF OURSELVES.

1. **Before this suffering, did you believe that God would ever give you more than you could handle?** How have your views changed now? How has it affected your relationship with Christ?

2. **Have either of you bought into the idea of self-sufficiency?** How has this grief forced you to come face-to-face with your limitations?

3. **What areas of life do you need to have a daily declaration of dependence on Christ?** Encourage each other to give those areas to Christ.

1. **Take a moment to acknowledge** and articulate to God how you have strived for independence and self-sufficiency rather than bringing your pain to him.

2. **If you can do so genuinely, invite God to help you let go and surrender self-sufficiency, trusting that his grace is fully sufficient for you.** If you're not there yet, pray that the days and weeks ahead will help move you closer to that and closer to him.

3. **Personalize and pray the following,** and feel encouraged to add anything else that you'd like to tell God. If you feel comfortable doing so, you could hold hands and do this together.

God, I recognize that you are strong, even and especially when I am weak.

I confess that I'm prone to mask that weakness and rely on my own strength.

Help me to surrender control and humbly depend on you in this season.

Help me decrease so that your power may increase in my life.

As I choose to abide in you, I trust that you will make me fruitful.

One day at a time.

Amen.

JUST ME AND JESUS?

SCRIPTURE

"For just as each of us has one body with many members, and these members do not all have the same function, so in Christ we, though many, form one body, and each member belongs to all the others."
—Romans 12:4–5

"Instead, speaking the truth in love, we will grow to become in every respect the mature body of him who is the head, that is, Christ. From him the whole body, joined and held together by every supporting ligament, grows and builds itself up in love, as each part does its work."
—Ephesians 4:15–16

There are plenty of solo sports out there, where an athlete is able to compete alone. We may be tempted to view the Christian life in that light. But once we choose to accept that Jesus is the way, the truth, and the life personally (John 14:6), it is critical that we also accept that he intends for us to live *communally*. The "just me and Jesus" approach to your faith can have the best of intentions, but it will not have the best of results on your faith, especially when you are walking through sorrow and suffering.

Cultural Myth: I am alone and no one else could possibly understand.

Biblical Truth: Comfort can be found in Christ and the Body of Christ.

A TEAM SPORT

While our walk with Jesus should always be deeply personal, it should never be completely private. If we retreat inward rather than opening outward, we are depriving ourselves of one of the most fundamental provisions the Lord has blessed us with: his people. Hebrews 10:24–

25 says, "And let us consider how we may spur one another on toward love and good deeds, not giving up meeting together, as some are in the habit of doing, but encouraging one another—and all the more as you see the Day approaching."

Christianity is not a solo sport, friends. In every way, the Christian journey is designed to be a team sport. We are called to train together and lean on each other, united by the greatest mission imaginable: to know God and enjoy his goodness now and forevermore. While our "forevermore" is eternally secure in Christ, our experience of his goodness here and now will be largely determined by the "teammates" we surround ourselves with. As the psalmist says, "How good and pleasant it is when God's people live together in unity" (Psalm 133:1).

A PAINFUL, BEAUTIFUL CYCLE

You're likely in a season where you feel empty, dry, and broken. One of the most profound things about availing yourself to others through the ups and the downs of life is that you will inevitably switch seats along the way. Others have walked before you through the valley of the shadow of death and others will come behind you. For the family of God, this sorrowful cycle brings about a beautiful opportunity. "Praise be to the God and Father of our Lord Jesus Christ, the Father of compassion and the God of all comfort, who comforts us in all our troubles, so that we can comfort those in any trouble with the comfort we ourselves receive from God. For just as we share abundantly in the sufferings of Christ, so also our

> CHRISTIANITY IS NOT A SOLO SPORT, FRIENDS. IN EVERY WAY, THE CHRISTIAN JOURNEY IS DESIGNED TO BE A TEAM SPORT.

comfort abounds through Christ" (2 Corinthians 1:3–5).

So when we endure life's hardships and thereby share in Christ's sufferings, we will also share in Christ's comfort. And after we share in Christ's comfort, we will find that we have a powerful opportunity to pass it on to others in his name. We can steward our sufferings as conduits of his grace, allowing his comfort to flow through us and spill over into the lives of others who are hurting.

We will never forget talking with Anne and Nate as they met us in the midst of our pain after they had lost their sweet Ava a few years prior. We had them write a guest post for our ministry's blog page. Here is an excerpt that sums up this painfully beautiful cycle:

> As we continue to walk through more and more of life, we are learning that pain is a universal human experience that transcends our specific circumstances. Whether or not you've ever lost a child, we have all experienced deep hurt and anguish, and we all know that life can be unspeakably hard. We're finding that the specific place of our very deepest pain and despair from our journey with Ava has become the well from which we can draw the purest waters of compassion, empathy, and love for those around us. Even if our particular griefs look incredibly different from one another, our point of pain has become the place from which we can enter into another's brokenness. We are well-acquainted with sorrow, but we are well-acquainted with the richness that is found there. And because of that, we can sit with the hurting and offer our presence as a tiny yet tangible picture of our Father's promise to be near to the brokenhearted (Psalm 34:18). What a beautiful privilege.

A FINAL EXHORTATION

We want to enter into the halfway point of this workbook with an exhortation to intentionally identify and courageously seek out safe people in your life to talk to and process with. If you don't have a preexisting support network, we'd humbly encourage you to pursue biblical community through a local body of believers.

We can guarantee you that there's no perfect church, or pastor, or small group, or support group. In the absence of perfection, we are still called to "Carry one another's burdens, and in this way you will fulfill the law of Christ" (Galatians 6:2), even if your brothers and sisters stub their toe and drop that weight from time to time. We genuinely believe that having people around you who know and love the Word of God can transform this season and transform your life. Comfort can always be found in Christ and the Body of Christ, and we pray you will come to experience this personally. You are not alone.

1. **Are either of you tempted to believe that you are alone in this suffering?** Do you retreat inward instead of accepting intentional community?

2. **Where are you at in the cycle of comfort? In what ways have you felt specifically comforted by others?** Have you been able to turn that comfort around to another hurting person? If not, encourage each other to be open to God using you in that way.

3. **Who are the safe people in your life?** What are your plans to include them in your journey of suffering?

4. **What does community and fellowship look like for each of you?** Are you actively plugged into a body of believers?

1. **Take a moment to acknowledge** and articulate to God if you have undervalued the presence and power of his people in your life.

2. **If you can do so genuinely, invite God to connect you with a healthy body of believers that can help bear your burdens and build you up.** If you're not there yet, pray that the days and weeks ahead will help move you closer to that and closer to him.

3. **Personalize and pray the following,** and feel encouraged to add anything else that you'd like to tell God. If you feel comfortable doing so, you could hold hands and do this together.

God, you alone are enough for us, but you don't call us to live alone.

We acknowledge that our faith is personal, but shouldn't be private.

Thank you for designing us to live among "teammates" who will spur us on.

Thank you for redeeming our pain, turning the comforted into comforters.

I ask for the courage to seek out and avail myself to a biblical community.

Help us not to neglect connecting and meeting with your people.

One day at a time.

Amen.

"

We can steward our sufferings as conduits of his grace, allowing his comfort to flow through us and spill over into the lives of others who are hurting.

WEEK THREE

RELATIONAL ROADBLOCKS

"

As we navigate this road of suffering, the various people in our lives might respond differently than we'd expect.

You have officially reached the halfway point of this workbook. We know that diving into your hurt as a couple hasn't been easy, but we pray it's been helpful.

Up to this point, we've explored a number of big questions and biblical beliefs at the theological level. We hope that the past two weeks' worth of devotion and reflection have shaped or reshaped your view of God in the midst of your circumstances and your sufferings, but we also pray that greater knowledge will not be the only outcome as we finish out this workbook. Keep pressing in together!

ON THE ROAD

Suffering can be "out of sight, out of mind" until it hits you. It seems like people rarely share publicly about their suffering, and the Church rarely speaks to the topic despite the material the Bible has for us. For those reasons and more, we often don't have a gauge on how to suffer well. We've often described seasons of suffering as a journey we're on, or a road we're navigating. The challenge is that it's like a road trip to a place you've vaguely heard about but never been to. You don't have a definitive address, and you don't have an iPhone to tell you when and where to turn next.

If you feel unequipped and overwhelmed on this journey of suffering, you're not the only one. Along the way, roadblocks are inevitable. You will take wrong turns and have to change course. There will be unexpected delays, and maybe even a wreck or two. You may just feel like you are utterly alone in unmarked terrain with no other cars in sight. No matter what, the entire experience is going to be difficult and demand more from you than you've become accustomed to.

Now imagine that you're not alone in that car. You have a copilot. You have some little passengers in the back. You even have a caravan of other vehicles behind you, wanting to be a part of this experience with you. It's a blessing to know you don't have to figure everything out by yourself. But with those people comes pressure. You may not be on the same page as your spouse riding shotgun. The kids are still requiring the same level of attention. Suddenly, managing these relational interactions can begin to feel like an additional burden on an already-difficult journey.

PEOPLE IN PURSUIT

In addition to seeking out fellowship with other Christ-followers who will encourage and remind you of God's truth, there are other relationships you will be responsible for; relationships where you are called husband or wife, mom or dad, son or daughter, brother or sister, boss or employee. The reality is that all of these relationships have different dynamics, but the one common thread is that they all consist of people who are human and therefore far from perfect. Relationships are complex and require a lot of intentionality to be healthy in any season. Overlay them with suffering, and they can become much more difficult, stressful, and taxing. Furthermore, whether we embrace it or resist it, the Lord is changing us through suffering, which will surely impact how we relate to the people in our lives.

As we navigate this road of suffering, the various people in our lives might respond differently than we'd expect. Sometimes they can exceed our expectations in a good way, and other times they can fail to meet our expectations in any number of ways. Some folks will have no idea what to say or do, and therefore choose to say and do nothing. Others will try to care for us, but the things they say and do may be more hurtful than helpful.

CHARTING THE COURSE

In this third week, we will focus on how to walk through this journey of suffering alongside the important people in our lives. Specifically, we will anticipate and explore five different relational roadblocks you both are likely to face, if you haven't already. As we do so, our first goal is for you to simply be aware of these potential "roadblocks." We don't want you to be surprised if you run into these different challenges in this season. Then, we want to help keep you from getting stuck in these relational ditches as you navigate your relationships amidst suffering. We hope to provide you with perspectives and practical handle-holds that will empower you to honor God and honor the important people in your lives.

Our aim over the next several days is to equip and encourage you with practical and applicable content. As we do so, our ultimate prayer is that you will experience peaceful, safe, supportive, and healthy relationships with your spouse, your children, your extended family and friends, and ultimately your Creator. We invite you to "buckle up" as we anticipate some of these new bumps in the road together.

SOCIALIZATION

"If either of them falls down, one can help the other up. But pity anyone who falls and has no one to help them up." —Ecclesiastes 4:10

"Whoever isolates himself seeks his own desire; he breaks out against all sound judgment." —Proverbs 18:1 ESV

"He says, 'Be still and know that I am God.'" —Psalm 46:10a

The first relational roadblock in suffering is socialization. It can be hard to strike a good balance in determining what it looks like to be around people, particularly when you are grieving. Who? When? Where? How often? This roadblock presents two different ditches that people are prone to fall into: on one side there is isolation, and on the other side there is busyness.

Walking alongside grieving families on a weekly basis, Kelly and I have seen that this roadblock is often a primary predictor of how moms and dads are doing as individuals and as a couple. As we explore both of these ditches, consider which one is more descriptive of you. We leaned in opposite directions here, as we'll share below, but talking through this roadblock really helped our marriage and our other relationships. It allowed us to better understand and empathize with each other's struggles and be more aware and sensitive to one another's needs. Ultimately, navigating this socialization roadblock together gave us the opportunity to consider, encourage, challenge, and serve one another.

AN INSTINCT TO ISOLATE

For some people, there is a strong desire to turn inward when they are hurting. I found myself trying to preserve what little emotional energy I had, and the thought of being around others elicited stress. I often felt like I literally wouldn't be able to carry on a conversation. I was failing to embrace God's provision for me through his people and my actions showed that I didn't necessarily believe that community was essential.

Over time, I discovered that whenever I pushed myself to engage with people who loved me, I would leave feeling filled up and encouraged. This doesn't mean I said yes to every invitation, but I consciously determined who I felt comforted and supported by, and I chose to entrust myself to their care and counsel. We are always and invariably healthier, stronger, and better with people around us to call us out of darkness and gently point us back to God's truth when we doubt and forget his words.

> "SELF-CARE" SHOULD BE A SUPPLEMENT TO BIBLICAL COMMUNITY, BUT NEVER A SUBSTITUTE FOR IT.

There are some days where you should absolutely get a pedicure with your earbuds in. "Self-care" should be a supplement to biblical community, but never a substitute for it. It is okay for our circle of people to get smaller in seasons of suffering, and it is okay to acknowledge that your capacity for social interaction has gone down. But it is never wise to isolate.

> NO AMOUNT OF BUSYNESS CAN MEND WHAT HAS BEEN BROKEN.

DANIEL

A BENT TOWARD BUSYNESS

For other people, there is a strong desire to turn outward when they are hurting, seeking refuge in social settings or work environments. I'd like to say that I did this purely because of the high value I place on people, but that's not what I was doing. I was using socialization as an escape and a welcomed distraction from grief. I'm often disastrously devoted to numbing out and ignoring hard things, so filling my schedule after Abel died was a coping mechanism that enabled my tendency to avoid and withdraw.

As simply as I can put it, I don't like to feel sad. I didn't want to sit in the sorrow, so I sought out "happiness" in the form of activities and engagements. This approach was effective at making me feel better for a period of time, but it did nothing to resolve the true issue at hand. The reality is that this particular "need for people" can never be satisfied, because no amount of busyness can mend what has been broken. Ironically, it can make us less present for the people we actually need and those who truly need us.

For extroverts, social interaction is a major source of life and health, even in suffering. By all means, surround yourself with loved ones, but challenge yourself to let those relationships be a place of authenticity rather than a time filler in your desire to avoid pain. And even so, remember to make time for yourself. In the early days of suffering, we have to also learn the value of solitude and get comfortable with being alone with our thoughts. We have to feel, even when the feelings hurt. It's all about balance. There are some days where you should go to that game night or birthday party. However, remember to check yourself. If you repeatedly run to social settings as a distraction, seeking solitude rather than constant interaction is my challenge to you.

A PATH FORWARD

Know yourself. First, self-identify with which ditch you're more than likely to fall into. Do an honest heart assessment of which way you're more likely to lean, and ask yourself why. If it's unclear to you, ask your spouse to graciously share any observations.

Establish healthy rhythms. Reevaluate your schedules. Determine if you need to ask for any of your commitments back. If you have a different ditch than your spouse, talk about how you can collectively land on a more centered approach to socialization. Find a middle ground!

When appropriate, challenge yourself. When we choose to press into discomfort, we often find that it can lead to our growth and be for our good. If you lean toward isolation, find times to intentionally say yes to social outings. And if you lean toward busyness, find times to intentionally say no to social outings.

Leverage accountability. Communicate the above to your core community. Let trusted people know what you've discussed and where you've landed together. Give them license to check in, to speak in, and to press in. This is and will be a great gift on your journey.

Despite our personal differences, we found that identifying and discussing this roadblock really helped our individual walks, our intimacy in marriage, and our healthy engagement with loved ones amidst suffering. Avoid the ditches of isolation and busyness, be fully present with one another, and be fully processing with one another.

1. **Who were you both before this journey of suffering?** Were you the one to always plan or be involved in a social gathering (extrovert), or would you rather spend your nights in (introvert)? Discuss together.

2. **Who are you both now?** Has this road of suffering caused you to be more outward or inward focused? Where do you see your natural bent as a help or hindrance in your healing? Discuss together.

3. **Name your socialization temptation.** If you are tempted to isolate, make a plan for a meaningful "yes" on your calendar. If busyness is your temptation, plan for a meaningful "no" on your calendar. Discuss these together and hold each other accountable.

4. **Encourage each other in healthy socialization.** Share stories of how God has worked through your surrounding community to bring comfort and also share times where God has used alone time to heal parts of your heart.

GUIDED PRAYER

1. **Take a moment to acknowledge** and articulate to God the ways you have hit the socialization roadblock.

2. **Invite God to help you see the importance of healthy socialization with your spouse and community.** Open your hearts to a healthier view of community.

3. **Personalize and pray the following,** and feel encouraged to add anything else that you'd like to tell God. If you feel comfortable doing so, you could hold hands and do this together.

God, you alone can meet our deepest needs.

Thank you for the gifts of your Word, your Spirit, and your people.

Give me wisdom in how to balance socialization and solitude in this season.

Help me avoid the ditches of isolation and busyness.

I desire to prioritize and pursue my relationship with you and with loved ones.

One day at a time.

Amen.

COMMUNICATION

SCRIPTURE

"Do not repay anyone evil for evil. Be careful to do what is right in the eyes of everyone. If it is possible, as far as it depends on you, live at peace with everyone."
—Romans 12:17–18

"Blessed are the peacemakers, for they will be called children of God . . . Therefore, if you are offering your gift at the altar and there remember that your brother or sister has something against you, leave your gift there in front of the altar. First go and be reconciled to them; then come and offer your gift."
—Matthew 5:9, 23–24

"Fools find no pleasure in understanding but delight in airing their own opinions. To answer before listening—that is folly and shame." —Proverbs 18:2, 13

The second relational roadblock in suffering is communication. The goal of communication is always mutual understanding. In seasons of suffering, seeking to understand one another will be as critical as ever—and as challenging as ever. Some days, you may feel like you're on a flip phone out in the country. The connection is spotty at best, and you're having trouble hearing one another clearly, or at all. Low signal. No Wi-Fi. It quickly becomes incredibly frustrating for both parties.

Communicating wants, needs, preferences, and desires is a huge and foundational part of all relationships. In this time, don't be surprised if it's much more difficult to identify those things, much less clearly communicate them to others. Oftentimes, in seasons of sorrow, we hit this roadblock because we haven't taken the proper time to process and reflect. For us, it felt like there weren't always words to sufficiently express how we were feeling, and sharing hard things felt vulnerable and tiresome. For one reason or another, as we suffer, our level of communication will likely suffer as well.

COMMUNICATION IN MARRIAGE

All of the above is true in most of our relationships, but we'll take a moment to speak specifically to husbands and wives. The covenant of marriage is a beautiful gift with unmatched potential for unity and security, but it's really hard to feel connected to your spouse when you're not communicating well. And it's hard to communicate well when you haven't been able to process your thoughts and feelings. Hence our dilemma.

It was incredibly beneficial for us to speak with another couple about this early on in our journey through suffering. While we were feeling strongly united at the time, they told us that we may not feel that way every single day. They shared that we probably wouldn't process pain in the exact same way and that there is grace and room for those differences. Ultimately, they taught us that the expectation is not that we will always match each another emotion-for-emotion, but that we'd know we were on the same team even if we weren't on the exact same page.

> "Search me, God, and know my heart; test me and know my anxious thoughts. See if there is any offensive way in me, and lead me in the way everlasting."
> —Psalm 139:23–24

There is a practice that has helped us facilitate communication and foster oneness that we'd highly recommend: a weekly check-in with each other. Set aside a recurring time to intentionally reflect, evaluate, and connect with one another. When done thoughtfully and consistently, questions like, "How are you feeling this week?" and "What has God been teaching you this past week?" or "What does your upcoming week look like and how can I pray for you?" can help you build unity and intimacy with your spouse on a routine basis.

COMMUNICATION IN CONFLICT

Any time we are communicating or relating to others, there will inevitably be disagreements and conflict. Resolving conflict can be hard in general, but when you're suffering, you may not feel like you have the emotional resources available to do it well or at all. Don't be surprised if words are weightier and wound easier. You're likely feeling more sensitive in general, and therefore more sensitive to anything that feels like criticism. Relationships that already require a lot of you can feel downright impossible to engage in when you are walking through suffering.

Depending on how you've seen conflict handled throughout your life, some of us are tempted to *fake* peace by passively withdrawing and sweeping things under the rug. But when you avoid healthy confrontation, you also avoid an opportunity for growth. Others might be tempted to *break* peace by escalating, invalidating, and seeking to dominate the other. But if you feel like you "won" and they "lost," you both just lost. The more fruitful—but admittedly more difficult—route is to make peace.

As we seek to resolve conflict and be reconciled, mutual understanding remains the goal of these conversations. Don't aim only to be heard and get your point across, aim to listen, seeking to understand before seeking to be understood. The first and most important step in this process is looking into our own hearts. It's easy to identify the ways we have felt hurt or frustrated, but it is far more difficult to spot our own sin and see our part in the problem. As we prayerfully search our hearts and own our parts, entering into conflict gently and graciously, it sets the tone and shapes the trajectory of everything that follows. Humility looks good on absolutely everybody. Approaching conflict with this posture even when you are hurting will bless your life and your relationships.

Stay engaged in the important relationships in your life, even when you're feeling weary. Be open and process with one another, even when you're feeling vulnerable. Pursue unity with one another, even when you're feeling distant. Believe the best in each other, even when you're feeling hurt. When we choose to communicate in an understanding way, we honor one another and we honor the Lord.

1. **How do you feel your communication is going with each other?** Do you feel like you are able to communicate clearly about your feelings and needs? If not, why do you think that is?

2. **Do you think a weekly check-in would be beneficial for you both?** If so, what day will you hold it on? What questions do you want to ask each other?

3. **Are you more tempted to be a peace faker or peace breaker?** What ways can you both work on to become peacemakers in this season especially?

4. **Commit to each other to spend time searching your own hearts today and this week.** Make it a goal this week to seek to understand each other more than you seek to be heard.

1. **Take a moment to acknowledge** and articulate to God the ways you have hit the communication roadblock.

2. **Invite God to help you see the importance of healthy communication with your spouse and others.** Open your hearts to a healthier view of communication in community.

3. **Personalize and pray the following,** and feel encouraged to add anything else that you'd like to tell God. If you feel comfortable doing so, you could hold hands and do this together.

God, I thank you for making peace with us when we were far from you.

I desire to pursue and honor others as I pursue and honor you.

Help me be open and authentic with my spouse and my community.

Help me seek mutual understanding more than I seek to be understood.

Help me to humble my heart and to own my part of any conflict.

Bless my relationships with unmatched depths of trust and unity as a result.

One day at a time.

Amen.

PARENTING

SCRIPTURE

"Start children off on the way they should go, and even when they are old they will not turn from it." —Proverbs 22:6

"Fathers, do not exasperate your children; instead, bring them up in the training and instruction of the Lord." —Ephesians 6:4

The third relational roadblock in suffering pertains to parenting and shepherding our children. Unfortunately, their needs won't cease because we're sad, and they probably won't modify their behavior out of respectful consideration either. You may have a harder time being present and staying engaged given the emotional, mental, and spiritual fatigue of this season, and less energy often leads to less patience. Furthermore, you are tasked with navigating your own pain as well as helping your other children process what's happening, particularly with older kids.

For these reasons and more, the prospect of guiding young hearts through hardship can feel like a daunting one. It is normal and natural for us as parents to want to protect our kids from pain and hardship, but the reality is that they *will* experience suffering in this life. Our task is to give them a lane to run in, and to teach them *how* to suffer well. The position you find yourself in as a parent will not be easy or straightforward, but it is an amazing opportunity for caregiving and discipleship.

COMFORTING OUR KIDS

Coping with suffering is difficult for everyone and different for everyone. Children, adolescents, girls, and boys all process emotions differently—

some through play, some through talking, while some choose to process internally. Depending on their age and stage of development, our children will have varying capacities for understanding, but they will all feel it in some way. One thing you can count on at any age is that your children are absorbing how you respond to a crisis, even if they appear to not be paying attention. Whether they fully comprehend the situation or not, the sorrow and grief you are carrying will inevitably impact and rub off on them.

"Love the Lord your God with all your heart and with all your soul and with all your strength. These commandments that I give you today are to be on your hearts. Impress them on your children. Talk about them when you sit at home and when you walk along the road, when you lie down and when you get up."
—Deuteronomy 6:5–7

For that reason, even in their limited understanding, we encourage you to have a foundational conversation with them. "This is going to be a very difficult time for our family. You may see me upset and cry, but I'm not upset with you. I love you very much! Feeling sad is normal and okay. If you feel like you want to cry, that's okay too. It's okay for us to show and share our pain. It's okay for you to always talk to me about these feelings." In times where your own energies and emotions are drained, it can be difficult to find the right words. Have grace with yourself and your spouse; this is incredibly hard for any parent. Even without words, showing physical affection toward them can communicate a lot and be a huge comfort to your kids.

PRODIGAL CHILDREN

Sometimes, the source of our sorrows can come from under our own roof, stemming from the very people who are most precious to us. The truth is that children are a source of unmatched joy in our lives, but they can also become a source of unmatched hurt and hardship. In Jesus' famous parable of the prodigal son (Luke 15:11–32), we see a son forsake his parents to partake instead in a life of self-indulgent sin and rebellion.

In the story, the father watches and waits prayerfully for his son to repent and return, but he *does not* follow after him or try to protect him from the world. One of the most important things we can do when our children rebel is to resist the urge to always intervene. Parents should never support their child's rebellion, and they should never shield their child from its repercussions either. As hard as it is, the most gracious and loving thing we can do is allow our children to experience the sting of their self-inflicted wounds. This is sure to be a painful process for them and for you, but when carried out biblically, it is the best path to genuine healing and restoration.

Our role as parents is to partner with God in being responsible *to* our children. However, we are not responsible for their bad choices. It's important to realize that all rebellion is first and foremost against God's authority before it is manifested against a parent's authority. Just as God transcends us as the primary authority over our children, he also

It is important to tell the truth to children in an age-appropriate way and allow opportunities for their questions to be answered. Keep explanations short, simple, and truthful, and expect that they may need to be reiterated over and over again. Whenever possible, help frame the season you will be walking through together.

While it is difficult to see our children suffer, it can build resilience and insight into the deeper meaning of life. Walking through hardship can produce in them more compassion and empathy for other hurting people in their life as they grow up. You have a privileged role to play in teaching your children how to steward their suffering for the glory of God and the good of others.

AS WE GUIDE AND MOLD THE HEARTS OF OUR KIDS TO THE BEST OF OUR ABILITY, WE CAN FAITHFULLY PLACE THEIR LIVES IN GOD'S HAND.

transcends us as their primary loving overseer. We can point them to Christ, but we cannot save our children—only God can do that. As we guide and mold the hearts of our kids to the best of our ability, we can faithfully place their lives in God's hand.

PARENTING WITH PURPOSE

Be authentic in your own grief journey. Do not mistake hiding your emotions for "being strong." If you never talk about hard things or show emotion, children will not think it is okay to grieve. Acknowledge and address suffering with your kids.

RESOURCES

Guiding Your Child Through Grief, by Mary Ann Emswiler and James P. Emswiler

10 Steps For Parenting Your Grieving Children, by Anne Hatcher Berenberg, Ph.D., Vicki Scalzitti and Jack Cain

What Do We Tell the Children? Talking to Kids about Death and Dying, by Joseph M. Primo

TheWarmPlace.org. The Warm Place offers some excellent insights on their resources page.

"What Will I Tell the Children?", by Nebraska Medicine

1. **Are either of you having a hard time parenting during this season?** What aspects are particularly hard? Be honest with one another.

2. **How are your children coping with this time of sorrow and suffering?** What are you worried about for them? How have they seen you respond to this journey?

3. **Do you need to have an honest talk with your kids about the difficulty of this season?** What are some things you want to make sure you tell them? What will mom say and what will dad say?

4. **Is the source of your sorrow coming from a choice one of your children made?** If so, grieve that loss with your spouse, then read Luke 15:11–32 and pray over your child together.

5. **What do you hope your kids will learn in this season of suffering?** Whether a more abiding faith in Christ or a greater capacity for empathy, how are they seeing that modeled in each of you?

GUIDED PRAYER

1. **Take a moment to acknowledge** and articulate to God the ways you have hit a parenting roadblock.

2. **Invite God to help you see the importance of parenting with your spouse in this season.**

3. **Personalize and pray the following,** and feel encouraged to add anything else that you'd like to tell God. If you feel comfortable doing so, you could hold hands and do this together.

God, you are a good Father to me and to my children.

It is almost unfathomable to think that you love them even more than I do.

As I walk authentically with you, help me walk authentically with them.

Give me the awareness and the words to compassionately care for my kids.

Help me gently and graciously parent them as you parent me.

I trust that you can use this season to grow them and grow me as a parent.

One day at a time.

Amen.

ACCEPTING HELP

The fourth relational roadblock in suffering is accepting help from others. In this workbook, we have talked a lot about how relationships are a gift from God. But the thing about gifts is that they have to be received and opened or they go to waste. In the same way, if we fail to open ourselves up to the people in our lives and receive the assistance they long to provide, we are leaving an incredibly good gift wrapped up and stowed away.

Depending on how you're wired, this roadblock may hit you in a few different ways. You may genuinely feel like you don't "need help," though we love you enough to say that is never really the case. You may just be a private person who shies away from expressing your needs, or simply aren't sure how to express those needs. Or maybe anything that seems remotely like charity is a hit to your pride, and you feel far more at home as the helper rather than the recipient. However this roadblock hits you, we hope today will equip you with some tools to help bridge the gap between you and the loved ones who desire to support you in this difficult season.

SCRIPTURE

"For just as each of us has one body with many members, and these members do not all have the same function, so in Christ we, though many, form one body, and each member belongs to all the others."
—Romans 12:4–5

"Carry each other's burdens, and in this way you will fulfill the law of Christ." —Galatians 6:2

THE BODY OF CHRIST IN ACTION

Initially, it was very difficult to accept help because we weren't even sure what was most comforting and didn't really know what we needed. For that reason, questions like, "How can I help? What can I do?" were often hard to answer. When people said, "Call me if you need anything," we appreciated it, but rarely made that call. For that reason, it was a huge blessing when people would sense a need and then move to meet it without direct instruction. There's nothing like waking up to, "Coffee and pastries are on your doorstep. We love you." or "Your yard will be mowed this afternoon." One of the sweetest parts of that season was getting to see the Church be the Church, as the body of Christ used their God-given gifts, talents, and treasures to support us in ways we didn't even know to ask for.

"And let us consider how we may spur one another on toward love and good deeds, not giving up meeting together, as some are in the habit of doing, but encouraging one another—and all the more as you see the Day approaching."
—Hebrews 10:24–25

Even so, as you begin to learn what you truly find most helpful and comforting, you'll want to help guide and point people in the right direction. Practically speaking, beginning sentences with "we're learning that" or "we've loved when" can be an effective way to share those things. For example: "We're learning that it helps to call us first rather than getting a surprise knock on the door" or "We've loved when people drop off sweet notes and sweet treats on our porch!" Articulating those desires and preferences as they become clearer over time can help set your loved ones up for success.

We were thankful to have so many people who loved us and loved Abel, but it often felt overwhelming and draining to have to rearticulate heavy information to dozens of people after our sonograms and appointments. One thing that helped us circumvent this issue was leveraging mass communication. We chose to start a blog, but this could take the form of email, social media, and so on. Sending updates proactively and collectively allows your loved ones to feel informed and valued, while saving you precious time and emotional energy. Including specific prayer requests in your updates and inviting others to pray on your behalf is also a great way to engage and involve your tribe. It was a win-win for us, and we'd encourage you to consider this if you've felt a similar strain.

LEADING WITH A LIMP

Daniel: Before we wrap up, I wanted to offer an exhortation specifically to the men. I'll lead off by confessing that I care more about my image than I'd like to admit, and I am constantly trying to project myself as competently and confidently as possible. I don't like showing that I'm hurt, because it feels like weakness, and men aren't supposed to be "weak." However, as the leader of my family, if I didn't get a grip on that desire for self-sufficiency, I knew it would become a serious roadblock to my walk with the Lord, my wife, and my extended community.

We talked last week about how appearing weak and dependent grates against our culture and our nature. Just as an example, we have had nearly a hundred hurting families reach out to Abel Speaks for support over the past few years. Guess how many times we heard from the father first? Four. It's the wife 95 percent of the time who sends that first message. That doesn't mean that the men are completely absent, and we usually do get to connect with both parents, but my point is this: God has wired us to love our wives and lead in our homes, and leaders take initiative. Ironically, humbling ourselves is a primary way we "step up." You have an incredible opportunity in front of you to lead with a limp.

For men and women alike, as you work on accepting help from others, we hope you are also accepting help from the Lord. Through Jesus, we have access to the creator of the heavens and the earth. When we choose to engage with God and God's people, we will experience the gifts of his presence and his peace.

GOD HAS WIRED US TO LOVE OUR WIVES AND LEAD IN OUR HOMES, AND LEADERS TAKE INITIATIVE. IRONICALLY, HUMBLING OURSELVES IS A PRIMARY WAY WE "STEP UP."

1. **How are both of you at receiving or asking for help?** Do you have a hard or easy time with it? If hard, why do you think that is?

2. **What are some of the main reasons you don't ask for help?** Not sure what to ask? Start to make a list together of very practical things and who in your community might meet them.

3. **Do you have a community that will simply drop everything and pray for your family?** Who are the first faces that come to mind if you need something?

4. **Husband, are you leading in asking and receiving help during this time?** Ask your wife how she feels you are doing in that area. What steps can you take to lead well in this area?

5. **How do you receive help from the Lord?** Help each other to turn to God first with all your needs and watch how he answers prayers through your community.

1. **Take a moment to acknowledge** and articulate to God any ways you have struggled to accept and receive help from others.

2. **Invite God to help you see the importance of a loving community and open yourself up to their support.**

3. **Personalize and pray the following,** and feel encouraged to add anything else that you'd like to tell God. If you feel comfortable doing so, you could hold hands and do this together.

> *God, you are the father of all comfort and the giver of every good gift.*
>
> *Thank you for the ways your people can remind me of your presence.*
>
> *Help me process the ways I feel most cared for and invite others into this journey.*
>
> *Help me repent and turn from my desire for self-sufficiency.*
>
> *I ask you to humble my heart to rely on the people you've blessed me with.*
>
> *I pray that I will see them as a daily reminder of your kindness and goodness.*
>
> *One day at a time.*
>
> *Amen.*

EMPATHY

"Praise be to the God and Father of our Lord Jesus Christ! In his great mercy he has given us new birth into a living hope through the resurrection of Jesus Christ from the dead, and into an inheritance that can never perish, spoil, or fade. This inheritance is kept in heaven for you, who through faith are shielded by God's power until the coming of the salvation that is ready to be revealed in the last time. In all this you greatly rejoice, though now for a little while you may have had to suffer grief in all kinds of trials." —1 Peter 1:3–6

SCRIPTURE

"Praise be to the God and Father of our Lord Jesus Christ, the Father of compassion and the God of all comfort, who comforts us in all our troubles, so that we can comfort those in any trouble with the comfort we ourselves receive from God. For just as we share abundantly in the sufferings of Christ, so also our comfort abounds through Christ."
—2 Corinthians 1:3–5

Our final relational roadblock pertains to our ability to extend empathy in suffering. You may find it frustrating when you hear friends complain or express worry about things that now feel trite, unimportant, or "just not that hard." Our hearts can harden toward circumstances that suddenly seem trivial in light of what you have been going through. However, if you are able to overcome this roadblock, it can turn into one of the greatest assets any Christ-follower can possess. By the grace of God, it's possible for our suffering to become a catalyst for extending and exuding empathy to others. You may just find that you are able to love people in a whole new way and on a whole new level, genuinely desiring to comfort them with the comfort you've received. That is where we hope to challenge you both today.

> BY THE GRACE OF GOD, IT'S POSSIBLE FOR OUR SUFFERING TO BECOME A CATALYST FOR EXTENDING AND EXUDING EMPATHY TO OTHERS.

DANIEL

NEW EYES

A small blessing we receive in suffering is the ability to home in on what matters most in this world. God gives us new eyes and a new perspective. We can no longer see the world as we once did. Some things that used to attract our attention have lost their appeal, and other things that played the background now stick out. Life's fleeting inconveniences slip into irrelevance, while those of eternal significance take their proper place in the forefront of our minds. If we allow it, our suffering has the power to transform the way we view this world and everything in it, helping us experience the reality that the classic hymn offers:

Turn your eyes upon Jesus.

Look full in his wonderful face,

And the things of earth will grow strangely dim,

in the light of his glory and grace.

KELLY

NEW HOPE

What Daniel is saying is that as we walked the road of suffering, we began to see things in light of eternity. As a result, the hope of heaven never felt more real to us. I'm embarrassed to admit it, but for most of my teens and twenties, if you would have asked me about Christ returning, my honest thoughts would have been, "Well sure, that's going to be awesome, but there's a lot I want to do and experience before then!" It's a strange and powerful thing to finally arrive in a place of genuinely desiring the Lord's return; like today, I'm ready! Jesus will bring heaven back down to earth—no more suffering, no more sorrow, and no more sadness; eternity in the presence of our Creator and Savior.

And even though I am ready, I know while on earth we still have the opportunity, and I believe the responsibility, to point others to that same eternal perspective that God has shown us through our sufferings. The Scriptures remind us that our life on earth is "a mist that appears for a little while and then vanishes" (James 4:14). As we suffer and struggle in this world, we begin to truly yearn and ache for the world to come, perhaps for the first time. In the scope of eternity, we are here for the blink of an eye, and for such a short period. Could it be that God wants to redeem your pain for his purposes, to help others have eternal hope in the midst of their suffering? Your ability to overcome the empathy roadblock may become your greatest tool for gospel ministry.

NEW HEARTS

At the most foundational levels, I am sure you have already found that suffering changes you into different people than you were before. We are given new eyes, a new hope, and Lord willing, we will have a new heart for the people around us. People who might not have lived through what we have, but are hurting nevertheless. Our calling, and our privilege, as believers is to be able to meet hurting people right where they are, validate their pain, and share with them the hope of the gospel. We get to be the hands and feet of Jesus as we "mourn with those who mourn" (Romans 12:15) and steward our suffering for the glory of God and the good of his children.

We've seen the ways that our suffering has the power to put up roadblocks in our relationships, but we've also seen that our suffering has the power to break down barriers and transform our relationships not only with God but with others. We have a choice: our pain and hardship can either become an obstacle to showing understanding and grace, or a catalyst that allows us to extend empathy in a whole new way. We pray that this difficult season will expand your view of eternity and your capacity to care for people. May the pain of your wounds become a balm to the wounds of others, for this life and the life to come.

OUR CALLING, AND OUR PRIVILEGE, AS BELIEVERS IS TO BE ABLE TO MEET HURTING PEOPLE RIGHT WHERE THEY ARE, VALIDATE THEIR PAIN, AND SHARE WITH THEM THE HOPE OF THE GOSPEL.

1. **Have there been times when your heart feels hardened toward others' stories of pain?** Talk about this with your spouse. How did it make you feel?

2. **Do either of you feel like you are at a place to be able to extend empathy to someone who is hurting?** If not, what is getting in the way?

3. **How have you felt cared for and comforted by your community and God?** Are you at a place where you feel you can comfort others in those ways? Be honest. It's okay if you're not there yet.

4. **What do you think it would look like for you both personally to share the Gospel through your story of suffering?** Have you had the opportunity to do that up to this point? If so, share stories to encourage each other. If not, what parts of your journey with God through suffering could be an encouragement to someone else?

GUIDED PRAYER

1. **Take a moment to acknowledge** and articulate to God if you have struggled with the roadblock of empathy.

2. **If you can do so genuinely, invite God** to give you a soft heart that extends grace and empathizes with people's pain. If you're not there yet, pray that the days and weeks ahead will help move you closer to that and closer to him.

3. **Personalize and pray the following,** and feel encouraged to add anything else that you'd like to tell God. If you feel comfortable doing so, you could hold hands and do this together.

God, you have shown such kindness and patience
toward your people.
Thank you for the way you move toward those who are hurting.
Thank you for using our suffering to change us for the better.
Give us new eyes drawn to what truly matters in this life.
Fuel an unceasing hope for heaven in our hearts.
Help us rejoice with those who rejoice and mourn with those
who mourn.
In all of these things, help me know Jesus and make Jesus known.
One day at a time.
Amen.

WEEK FOUR

PURPOSE IN THE PAIN

"

If you stay in awareness and conversation with yourself, your spouse, and your God, you will find the season that is to come to be one of the most life-giving and rewarding experiences of your life.

"God has a purpose for every obstacle and every frustration and every pain and every affliction . . . Whatever else God may be doing at the planning level of our life, he is always doing things at the heart level of your life." —John Piper, *Called to Suffer and Rejoice*

Kelly and I are so thankful to Bethlehem Baptist Church and John Piper for their series named *Called to Suffer and Rejoice* given in 1992. It has given us a lot of comfort and perspective as we have walked the road of suffering.

Before we started our ministry, Abel Speaks, I (Daniel) directed a college ministry for eighteen- to twenty-two-year-olds in Dallas. One of the young men I met and will never forget is Brandon. With his permission, I'd love to share a part of his story.

"BECAUSE OF MY ILLNESS"

Growing up, Brandon was a typical healthy kid until the summer of 2008, when he began losing his ability to communicate and perform basic physical tasks. His parents were watching their son slowly deteriorate before their eyes. They discovered that Brandon has a muscle disorder called dystonia, and the next several years were marked by appointments, therapies, and a brain stimulation surgery. "I wrestled with God," Brandon's mom shared. "Why us? Why our son? What have we done? I remember one quiet time where I finally broke down, literally bawling on my hands and knees. I called my husband and told him that we can't do this anymore. The anger, the ups and downs, we need to give it all to God. We had to accept that Brandon's life was ultimately in God's hands, not ours."

Brandon's resilience is impossible to put into words. By 2016, he had quickly become a staple within our ministry and our church. We took a spring break trip, and one night we were all gathered together, discussing what it means to have joy and reasons we have joy. I noticed Brandon typing a note on his phone, which he is able to do with great difficulty. He leaned over to show me the screen. It said: "I have joy because of my illness." Not in spite of his illness—because of his illness. I stopped and read his words aloud. I'll never forget that moment and the conversation it sparked in a room full of fifty college students. And I guarantee they haven't forgotten it either.

While his mind functions fully, his body does not, and his experience as a teenager and now a young adult in this world looks vastly different than his peers. On the surface, you might think that Brandon has been robbed of so many things. But at a heart level, he has gained something that most of his peers have not. And with wisdom beyond his years, Brandon recognizes this. There are plenty of days when Brandon thinks, "I'm ready for this to be over. I want God to take this away." But he knows God is using his illness in his life and the lives of others. There is purpose in his pain, and that's what keeps him going.

Brandon's mom continued: "We've had so many kids and so many parents come up and say, 'Your son just lights me up with that smile.' But Brandon wouldn't have that smile if he didn't know God had his back. People kind of look at you funny when you tell them you've been blessed by your child's disorder, which may realistically not have a cure. But it has been amazing to watch how his story has become a witness tool for God. Quite honestly, I wish I was more like him. And if it took dystonia to give me that kind of faith and that kind of power, then God, bring it on."

NEVER POINTLESS

Brandon's story frames this final week for us in so many ways. We may never know the reasons for our sorrows, but we can know without a doubt that our pain is never pointless. God does not delight in our suffering, but he does use it in powerfully profound ways if we let him.

In the words of Charles Spurgeon, "God is too good to be unkind, and too wise to be mistaken. When we cannot trace his hand, we must trust his heart. The sweetest prayers God ever hears are the groans and sighs of those who have no hope in anything but his love."

As we consider some of the many ways that God is redemptively at work for his glory and our good, we pray you will trust his heart even when you cannot trace his hand. We pray you will come to hope in our Father's love like you have never hoped before. And as a result, we pray that you might have joy just like Brandon's . . . not in spite of your sufferings, but because of them.

THE "GOOD" PURPOSE

"I've come to see that it's through the deepest suffering that God has taught me the deepest lessons. And if we'll trust Him for it, we can come through to the unshakable assurance that he's in charge. He has a loving purpose. And he can transform something terrible into something wonderful. Suffering is never for nothing." —Elisabeth Elliot, *Suffering is Never for Nothing*

SCRIPTURE

"Dear friends, *do not be surprised* at the fiery ordeal that has come on you to test you, as though something strange were happening to you. But rejoice inasmuch as you participate in the sufferings of Christ, so that you may be overjoyed when his glory is revealed." —1 Peter 4:12– 13 (emphasis added)

"For it is by grace you have been saved, through faith—and this is not from yourselves, it is the gift of God— not by works, so that no one can boast. *For we are God's handiwork,* created in Christ Jesus to do good works, which God prepared in advance for us to do." —Ephesians 2:8–10 (emphasis added)

Some Bible verses are more frequently quoted than others. Whether you're a Christian Bible reader or a church pastor, let's admit that it's far more enjoyable to emphasize the more pleasant passages and positive promises; the verses that fire us up and make us feel good. Speaking of that word, Romans 8:28 may be at the top of this list: "And we know that in all things God works for the *good* of those who love him, who have been called according to his *purpose*" (emphasis added).

If we're going to spend the week considering "his purposes," we must first understand what it means for God to "work for the good of those who love him." It's very clear that God is completely, unwaveringly devoted to his eternal glory and our ultimate good. It's much less clear how we reconcile this idea with our past scars and our present sorrows. As much as we'd like to condense life into two buckets, labeled "good" and "bad," I think we consistently find life's not that simple. And neither is God.

ROMANS 8, IN CONTEXT

Let's start with what Romans 8:28 *can't* mean. While God promises to work all things together for our good, there are dozens of passages where he also promises that we will suffer in this life. The apostle Paul wrote this verse, for crying out loud. This is the same man who almost obsessively

> GOD'S GREATEST PURPOSE AND ULTIMATE AIM
> FOR THOSE WHO LOVE HIM IS THAT WE WOULD
> BE CONFORMED TO THE IMAGE OF HIS SON.

talks about suffering for the gospel throughout his writings, and within Romans itself. Just eleven verses prior, we read, "Now if we are children, then we are heirs—heirs of God and co-heirs with Christ, if indeed we share in his sufferings in order that we may also share in his glory" (Romans 8:17). If you are a child of God and a follower Christ, you will share in his sufferings before you ever share in his glory. So Romans 8:28 is not telling us that the Christian life will be an easy one.

I believe the key to understanding the truth of Romans 8:28 begins with recognizing that our human definition of *good* is very, very different than God's definition. Thankfully, he tips his cards for us in verse 29. Let's read them both together and see what we find: "And we know that in all things God works for the good of those who love him, who have been called according to his purpose. For those God foreknew he also predestined to be conformed to the image of his Son, that he might be the firstborn among many brothers and sisters" (Romans 8:28–29).

Did you catch it? God's design for "working all things together for good"? God's greatest purpose and ultimate aim for those who love him is that we would be *conformed to the image of his Son*. We define *good* through the lens of our external life, found in our contentment and our circumstance. God defines good through the lens of our eternal life, found in our conformity to Christ. Ultimately, Romans 8:28–29 is telling us that there is no greater "good" than greater conformity to Christ.

A WORK IN PROGRESS

With all of that said, the most challenging time to see and trust God's definition of 'good' is when we're deep in the thick of our suffering. The wounds are fresh and relief seems so far off, if not entirely unattainable. Either way, there is just no taking the pain away and there is no avoiding the menacing question, "How could this *ever* be good?"

A mentor of mine once said, "If it's not good, God's not done." He didn't say it flippantly or ignorantly,

I promise. His point was simply that so often, the missing ingredient in our healing is *time*. I won't speak for you, but each year removed from saying goodbye to our son feels different. The pain is not erased, but it has evolved. Abel's absence has left a scar that will remain, but the wound is slowly mending. We may never see the full picture on this side of eternity, but I get the feeling that Abel's life and legacy is an unfinished painting; a work in progress that just may become a masterpiece.

You're likely familiar with the famous statue of David sculpted by brilliant Renaissance artist Michelangelo. I once heard a story that he was asked about the challenges of creating David from a single block of marble. As the story allegedly goes, Michelangelo replied, "It is easy. You just chip away all the stone that doesn't look like David." Where you are right now, things may not seem good, look good, or feel good. Our lives may feel like God is taking a hammer to a chisel, blow after blow after blow. It's rocky and it's raw and it's messy. There is debris all over the floor. But maybe, just maybe, God is in the process of creating something priceless that the world will marvel at. Maybe God is skillfully and masterfully doing something similar to Michelangelo: *"I'm going to chip away everything that doesn't look like Jesus."* In the end, the work of art is awe-inspiring, and the artist gets the glory.

GOOD FRIDAY

Have you ever stopped to think about the fact that Christians have chosen to call the day of Christ's crucifixion "Good Friday"? I don't know when this tradition began, but I wonder if his original disciples would have found it offensive and insulting. I mean, this is the day their leader and friend was publicly ridiculed and brutally murdered. A lot of words would come to mind for that Friday and Saturday, but I doubt "good" would be one of them. Hiding themselves and grieving the horrors of what had just happened to Jesus. Grappling with the ramifications

of his death after leaving absolutely everything behind to go all-in with him. Having their expectations of the Messiah die with him, and their perceived vision of his coming kingdom crumble to pieces.

What's so "good" about Good Friday? Because without a crucifixion on Friday, there is no resurrection on Sunday. Think about that. The single most horrific thing that has ever happened is eternally and inseparably tied to the greatest thing that has ever happened. It doesn't blot out the nail marks in our Savior's hands (John 20:25), but it does blot out our transgressions and iniquities (Psalm 51:1, 9). It doesn't empty the cross of its pain, but it does empty death of its sting. From something unspeakably ugly springs something beautiful beyond belief.

"Terrible day, not a terrible life. Hard season, but a beautiful story. Awful chapter, but an amazing book. Perspective is everything. The day Jesus died was simultaneously the worst and greatest day in history. It looked like death, but it gave me life."
—Luke Lezon

Suffering is not evidence that you are somehow outside of God's will or blessing. Jesus was right in the middle of God's will as he hung lifeless on a Roman cross, and God did not waste a drop of Christ's blood or an ounce of his pain. Resurrection Sunday was coming, and with it, salvation for all who would repent and believe. Romans 8:28 reminds us that even when we love and seek God, even and especially when life doesn't feel "good," you are no less at the center of God's will. He has you right where he wants you, working all things together for our highest good and his utmost glory.

RESURRECTION SUNDAY WAS COMING, AND WITH IT, SALVATION FOR ALL WHO WOULD REPENT AND BELIEVE.

1. **Are there any ways that you see God bringing about good from your suffering?** Any areas where you are experiencing greater conformity to Christ?

2. **Do you identify and empathize with how the disciples must have felt on Friday and Saturday?** How does knowing the way the story ends change the perspective with which we now view their days of sorrow? And how might this comfort you in the "Saturday" you are living right now?

3. **Can you think of an instance where you felt the Lord's kindness even on a really hard day?** (Example: Our son's memorial service was in mid-February, but God provided us with a warm sunny day to enjoy as we celebrated Abel's life.)

1. **Take a moment to articulate** to God why it feels so hard to see what "good" could ever come of your current sufferings.

2. **If you can do so genuinely, invite God to use this season sculpt you increasingly into the image of Christ.** If you're not there yet, pray that the days and weeks ahead will help move you closer to that and closer to him.

3. **Personalize and pray the following,** and feel encouraged to add anything else that you'd like to tell God. If you feel comfortable doing so, you could hold hands and do this together.

God, there's so much we just don't understand.

Help us believe you can work all things together for your glory and our good.

And help us trust you on the days when we inevitably struggle to do so.

Thank you for the good gift of Jesus' life, death, and resurrection.

Please comfort us as we await the glorious hope he has secured for us.

And in the meantime, please make us more and more like our Savior.

One day at a time.

Amen.

THE INTIMACY PURPOSE

DANIEL

SCRIPTURE

"For we do not have a high priest who is unable to empathize with our weaknesses, but we have one who has been tempted in every way, just as we are—yet he did not sin. Let us then approach God's throne of grace with confidence, so that we may receive mercy and find grace to help us in our time of need." —Hebrews 4:15–16

"The Son is the image of the invisible God, the firstborn over all creation . . . For God was pleased to have all his fullness dwell in him, and through him to reconcile to himself all things, whether things on earth or things in heaven, by making peace through his blood, shed on the cross." —Colossians 1:15, 19–20

In 2001, long before the days of Netflix and limitless on-demand digital streaming, there was an HBO miniseries that had everybody talking. It chronicled the exploits of Easy Company, an infantry unit of the US Army's 101st Airborne Division during World War II. There are plenty of reasons why people were so taken by this show, as it was produced by Tom Hanks and Steven Spielberg and won Emmy and Golden Globe awards. But more than anything, I believe what resonated most deeply is the fact that it was based on a true story of real-life heroes. Men who came from different places with different interests and different walks of life, but who became more than a military battalion. They became family. They became a *Band of Brothers*.

I start there today because it illustrates a powerful truth: When people endure suffering together, it connects them in a way that is beyond any other shared experience. The deepest bonds in life are forged in the foxhole.

FULLY GOD, FULLY MAN

Jesus is God, and yet, he is also God in the *flesh*. He lived a fully human experience as a young man. He experienced the full spectrum of thoughts and emotions. He laughed and he cried. He got tired, and hungry, and thirsty. He got frustrated. He grieved injustice. He worked with his hands a lot. He prayed, a lot. He had best friends and went to social gatherings with them. He drank wine. He engaged with poor people and was kind to those who could do nothing for him. He had parents and siblings that didn't always get him. He knew pure joy and deep pain. In short, he lived life.

> "He is infinite, and that answers our longing for completeness. He is eternal, and that answers our longing for permanence. He is unchangeable, and that answers our longing for stability and security. There is none like God. Nothing can compare with him. Wealth, sex, power, popularity, conquest, productivity, great achievement—nothing can compare with God." —John Piper, Desiring God

My point is that Jesus is not some detached divinity who can't comprehend what we're walking through. As the author of Hebrews writes, "For this reason he had to be made like them, *fully human in every way*, in order that he might become a merciful and faithful high priest in service to God, and that he might make atonement for the sins of the people. *Because he himself suffered when he was tempted, he is able to help those who are being tempted*" (Hebrews 2:17–18, emphasis added). If anyone knows human suffering, it's Jesus of Nazareth. And in that place we never desire to be, he always desires to meet us. To band together and believe that he has our back. And slowly but surely, to know him more deeply and trust him more fully.

JOINING CHRIST

Similar to what *Band of Brothers* demonstrated, we are consistently moved by the stories of courageous, faithful believers who have endured the greatest tragedies and persecutions. Often, we're impressed by the strength and resolve these men and women possess to overcome adversity. But do you know what leaves the biggest mark on me? Somehow, mysteriously, the people who seem to know God best are the people who suffer with Christ the most. It would appear that suffering is a pathway deep into the heart of God. We see it in testimony after testimony. Life is hard, but God is good. He is with us, and that's enough. There is a special revelation, a special intimacy, prepared for those who join Jesus in the trenches. We will truly know the power of Christ as we "share in suffering as a good soldier of Christ Jesus" (2 Timothy 2:3).

GREAT LOSS, GREATER GAIN

Paul speaks about this participation in Christ's sufferings in Philippians 3:7–11, where he also shows us that the greatest gains and pleasures this world has to offer are complete garbage compared to knowing Jesus. For him, finding and gaining an intimate relationship with Christ is the ultimate win in this life, and everything else sits in the loss column by comparison. Even as Paul underwent suffering in this life, he did not do so passively. He did so purposefully. And his purpose was to gain Christ. It flies in the face of how we naturally keep score, but apparently more suffering equals more Jesus.

> But whatever were gains to me I now consider loss for the sake of Christ. What is more, I consider everything a loss because of the surpassing worth of knowing Christ Jesus my Lord, for whose sake I have lost all things. I consider them garbage, *that I may gain Christ and be found in him*, not having a righteousness of my own that comes from the law, but that which is through faith in Christ—the righteousness that comes from God on the basis of faith. *I want to know Christ*—yes, to know the power of his resurrection *and participation in his sufferings*, becoming like him in his death, and so, somehow, attaining to the resurrection from the dead (Philippians 3:7–11, emphasis added).

Lest we think Paul was a special breed or a super-spiritual exception to the norm, six verses later he explicitly exhorts us to embrace and imitate this outlook. "Join together in following my example, brothers and sisters, and just as you have us as a model, keep your eyes on those who live as we do" (Philippians 3:17). This is normal Christianity. This is what following Jesus should look like, as individuals and as churches. We will never be strangers to suffering in this world. But in the midst of it, we can live as "strangers and exiles" in this world (1 Peter 2:11). Strange people who experience loss, but somehow seem to gain something greater in the process. Strange people who know Jesus more fully and connect with him more deeply as we faithfully share in his sufferings.

IF ANYONE KNOWS HUMAN SUFFERING, IT'S JESUS OF NAZARETH. AND IN THAT PLACE WE NEVER DESIRE TO BE, HE ALWAYS DESIRES TO MEET US.

1. **As you have both walked this road of suffering, would you say it has brought you closer to Jesus or farther away?** On a scale of 1–10, how would you both rate your intimacy with him in this season?

2. **How does knowing that Jesus was human and familiar with suffering shape your view of him?** Does he seem more relatable? Does that make it easier to connect with him and invite him into your experience?

3. **Have you ever considered the idea that you are actually sharing and participating in Christ's sufferings?** How might this concept change the way you are processing this experience?

4. **What are ways you can move toward deeper intimacy with Jesus, both individually and together?** What specific practices and perspectives can you incorporate into your daily lives?

5. **Do you believe that great pain can lead to greater possibility for intimacy with Christ?** How can this impact the way you are processing in this season?

1. **Take a moment to acknowledge** and articulate to God the ways that you have or have not sought intimacy with him in the midst of your suffering.

2. **If you can do so genuinely, tell him that you desire to know him better and connect with him more deeply, no matter the cost.** If you're not there yet, pray that the days and weeks ahead will help move you closer to that and closer to him.

3. **Personalize and pray the following,** and feel encouraged to add anything else that you'd like to tell God. If you feel comfortable doing so, you could hold hands and do this together.

God, we long to know you more deeply and trust you more fully.

We marvel at your humility to enter into the human experience.

We marvel that you willingly put on flesh and endure suffering just like us.

Help us to see you and to seek you in the valleys of this life.

Help us to see intimacy with you as the greatest gain attainable.

One day at a time.

Amen.

THE MATURITY PURPOSE

"We can experience growth and flourishing not just in spite of our sufferings, but because of them."
—Jay and Katherine Wolfe, *Suffer Strong*

SCRIPTURE

"Those who sow with tears will reap with songs of joy. Those who go out weeping, carrying seed to sow, will return with songs of joy, carrying sheaves with them."
—Psalm 126:5–6

"But you, keep your head in all situations, endure hardship, do the work of an evangelist, discharge all the duties of your ministry. For I am already being poured out like a drink offering, and the time for my departure is near. *I have fought the good fight, I have finished the race, I have kept the faith.* Now there is in store for me the crown of righteousness, which the Lord, the righteous Judge, will award to me on that day—and not only to me, but also to *all who have longed for his appearing.*" —2 Timothy 4:5–8, emphasis added

Kelly may be a CrossFit mama, but the gym has never been my happy place. For daddy, it's pickup sports or bust, but I've got two good friends who do Ironman triathlons. Yes, three continual and sequential endurance races. Voluntarily and on purpose. These guys go for a bold 2.4-mile swim, hop out of the water and onto a bicycle where they pedal for 112 miles, and then—just to top things off—they run a full 26.2-mile marathon. And! They actually *pay* money to partake in this madness! I don't get it.

HOLINESS AND HOPE

In a very real way, exercise and fitness is one example of how we actually can and do willfully choose to undergo suffering at certain times for certain purposes. For reasons we deem noble and worthy enough, we will put ourselves through the ringer. Not because we enjoy the pain, but because we desire what the pain produces in us. In a word, it leads to *growth*.

I recognize that the affliction most of us are walking through is very, very different than shortness of breath and sore muscles. But the truth remains. Our suffering will have spiritually maturing effects on our faith. God can use it for our growth, and therefore, our good. "Not only so, but we also glory in our sufferings, because we know that suffering produces perseverance; perseverance, character; and character, hope. And hope does not put us to shame, because God's love has been poured out into our hearts through the Holy Spirit, who has been given to us" (Romans 5:3–5).

I love how clearly and logically that progression is laid out for us. Suffering produces within us a perseverance, a patient endurance. This patient

"Sometimes God allows what he hates to accomplish what he loves." —Joni Eareckson Tada, The God I Love

endurance produces a proven character resulting in a stronger faith. And in the midst of our sorrows, when we hold onto him and find that he is holding onto us, it produces a heavenly hope that we couldn't have attained any other way. God is fully committed to increasing the hope and holiness of his people, and as we suffer faithfully, we'll find that he is able to accomplish those very things.

REVEALING AND REFINING

You may recall one of Jesus' most famous stories, the parable of the sower. As four seeds fall to the ground, the various results are meant to illustrate various responses to the call of Christ. In describing one of them, he says, "The seed falling on rocky ground refers to someone who hears the word and at once receives it with joy. But since they have no root, they last only a short time. When trouble or persecution comes because of the word, they quickly fall away" (Matthew 13:20–21). As we weather through the ups and downs of this world, Jesus is telling us that hardship will either validate that we are firmly planted and in the process of yielding much fruit, or prove that we were never truly rooted in him to begin with.

The apostle Peter used another word picture as he wrote: "In this you rejoice, though now for a little while, if necessary, you have been grieved by various trials, so that the tested genuineness of your faith— more precious than gold that perishes though it is tested by fire—may be found to result in praise and glory and honor at the revelation of Jesus Christ" (1 Peter 1:6–7). Suffering brings out the full measure of one's devotion, where we can actually *see* our commitment to Christ and *know* that we are truly his.

So the way we respond to our trials and tribulations will be incredibly revealing, but it's more than that. When that brick of gold goes into the furnace, the fire will test the precious metal's true substance. But once proven, the fire doesn't stop there. It *purifies* the gold. In the same way, suffering doesn't just reveal our faith—it *refines* it. The believer's faith was already genuine beforehand, but the flames burn away the dross and the impurities. We come out of the fire different than we went in. More resolved. More mature. More precious. We find that the furnace has transformed us for the better. Our suffering both reveals and refines our faith.

> ONCE PROVEN, THE FIRE DOESN'T STOP THERE. IT PURIFIES THE GOLD. IN THE SAME WAY, SUFFERING DOESN'T JUST REVEAL OUR FAITH—IT REFINES IT.

THE RACE AND THE REWARD

I texted my crazy friends after they finished their first triathlon to ask how they felt. One said, "It hurt— but it was kind of painful and also kind of euphoric." And the other said, "The next few days I was limping around and could barely bend my knees." Once again, it begs the question of why in the world they would subject themselves to that sort of struggling and discomfort. Then it hit me. At the same moment these men were in their *worst physical pain*, these men were also in the *best physical shape* of their lives.

Their training and their suffering had produced something, and not simply in the realm of fitness. It had produced a harvest of discipline, consistency, faithfulness, endurance, and maturity. This is what compelled Jesus' half-brother, James, to open his epistle the way he does: "Consider it pure joy, my brothers and sisters, whenever you face trials of many kinds, because you know that the testing of your faith produces perseverance. Let perseverance finish its work so that you may be mature and complete, not lacking anything" (James 1:2–4).

We don't rejoice in our sufferings because we like being miserable. We endure what we don't desire because it brings about what we *do* desire, to become mature and complete, not lacking anything. Because God is good, because he is producing something in us and we can consider it pure joy and give thanks even in the midst of our sorrow.

If the struggles of physical training will strengthen our bodies, how much more might the struggles of spiritual training strengthen our faith? As the apostle Paul exhorted his disciple Timothy, "Train yourself to be godly. For physical training is of some value, but godliness has value for all things, holding promise for both the present life and the life to come. This is a trustworthy saying that deserves full acceptance" (1 Timothy 4:7b-9). Suffering can and does have spiritually maturing effects on our faith, for God's ultimate glory and our ultimate good.

WE ENDURE WHAT WE DON'T DESIRE BECAUSE IT BRINGS ABOUT WHAT WE DO DESIRE, TO BECOME MATURE AND COMPLETE, NOT LACKING ANYTHING.

1. **The pathway of suffering can be long and tiring.** How are each of you feeling today?

2. **In the midst of this difficult season, are there things you can rejoice in and thank him for?** Consider any ways in the past week that the Lord has given you small glimmers of hope that have strengthened and spurred you on.

3. **Reread the progression that Paul walks through in Romans 5:3–5. Do you identify with any of those traits as a result of suffering?** Perseverance, character, hope, and so forth.

4. **Are there other ways that this season of suffering has grown and strengthened your "faith muscles"? Have you seen suffering purify and refine your faith?** For example, finding that your perspective on life is changing, gradually trusting the Lord more and more, experiencing his strength even in your weakness, desiring eternity with God in a new way, etc.

5. **Finally, if you're walking through this with your spouse,** I'd love to give you the opportunity to share your own observations and affirm them. In what ways have you seen your spouse grow over the past month?

GUIDED PRAYER

1. **Take a moment to acknowledge** and articulate to God any ways you feel you've been resisting spiritual growth.

2. **If you can do so genuinely, invite and allow God to use this season to produce within you a stronger, more resilient faith in him.** If you're not there yet, pray that the days and weeks ahead will help move you closer to that and closer to him.

3. **Personalize and pray the following,** and feel encouraged to add anything else that you'd like to tell God. If you feel comfortable doing so, you could hold hands and do this together.

> *God, it is painful, but we believe you are producing something good in us.*
>
> *We invite you to grow and mature us as you refine our faith.*
>
> *Help us endure what we don't desire and fully experience what you do desire.*
>
> *Help us stay firmly rooted and bear fruit for you in this season.*
>
> *Help us pursue godliness and run this race with perseverance.*
>
> *One day at a time.*
>
> *Amen.*

THE MINISTRY PURPOSE

SCRIPTURE

"To this you were called, because Christ suffered for you, leaving you an example, that you should follow in his steps." —1 Peter 2:21

"But we have this treasure in jars of clay, to show that the surpassing power belongs to God and not to us. We are afflicted in every way, but not crushed; perplexed, but not driven to despair; persecuted, but not forsaken; struck down, but not destroyed; always carrying in the body the death of Jesus, so that the life of Jesus may also be manifested in our bodies." —2 Corinthians 4:7–10

We once heard a story about a missionary who walked barefoot from place to place preaching the gospel in India. After one long day of arduous travel, he arrived at a village and tried to share about Christ but was consistently rejected and eventually driven out of town. Discouraged and dejected, he went to the edge of the village and laid down under a tree where he fell asleep from utter exhaustion.

When he awoke, he discovered that people were hovering over him. It seemed like the whole town had gathered around this tree. The leader of the village explained that they came to look him over while he was sleeping, and they saw his feet. Blistered, cut, bloodied, and swollen. They considered the pain and the hardship this man had endured on his journey, and it softened their hearts and tuned their ears to hear the message he had for them. There was something powerful about the way this man had sacrificed and suffered in the name of Jesus, and it paved the way for the gospel to truly resonate. He didn't just share with them the message of the cross, he had *shown* them the message of the cross.

THE CRUCIFORM LIFE

In the many ways we may describe following Jesus, one term has resonated with us ever since we heard it in a Bible Project video: "the cruciform life." Literally, the word *cruciform* means "in the shape of a cross." Thus, the cruciform life is a life shaped by the cross. Jesus himself said it this way: "If anyone would come after me, let him deny himself and take up his cross daily and follow me. For whoever would save his life will lose it, but whoever loses his life for my sake will save it" (Luke 9:23–24).

While Christians will typically recognize their call to imitate the life of Christ—his love, his humility, his generosity, and so on—they may be slower to embrace the fact that we are also called to imitate the *death* of Christ. God intends for the afflictions of Christ to be presented to the world through the afflictions of his people, the body of Christ. When God's people suffer faithfully, they embody and extend the message of the cross. This is what Paul is illustrating as he writes that believers are "always carrying in our body the *death* of Jesus, so that the *life* of Jesus may also be manifested in our bodies" (2 Corinthians 4:10, emphasis added). Christ's sufferings made salvation possible, and now our sufferings can make that message of salvation visible so that a watching world can actually see the hope of the gospel lived out in front of their very eyes.

> "Endurance amid affliction is the greatest display of God's presence, power, and glory in this fallen world." —John Piper, *Called to Suffer and Rejoice*

Every Christian should be living a cruciform life shaped by the cross. And while there may not be a *less desirable* way to do so, there may not be a *more impactful* way to share the hope of Christ than when we navigate suffering differently than people would ever expect and in ways they could never explain. For that reason, we contend that the suffering

WE BELIEVE THE SCRIPTURES SAY THAT OUR SUFFERING IS SOMETHING THAT GOD HAS ENTRUSTED TO US TO BE STEWARDED.

in our lives is not simply something that is randomly happening to us. We believe the Scriptures say that our suffering is something that God has *entrusted* to us to be stewarded. We believe it because we've seen it time and time again, and we'd love to close by sharing what this has looked like in our own story.

ABEL SPEAKS

Throughout Abel's life on earth, we'd get messages from Facebook friends we hadn't seen in years or friends-of-friends we'd never met telling us how connected they felt to our story and how moved they were by our journey. They had been watching. They had been impacted. But it wasn't until after Abel's passing that we realized the extent to which God planned to use his story and our suffering. One after another, moms and dads were finding and contacting us after receiving a life-limiting diagnosis for their own child. They were searching for advice, comfort, and support from someone who had walked a similar road. They were searching for hope in the midst of sorrow.

In January of 2018, on what would have been his second birthday, Abel Speaks (AbelSpeaks.org) was officially born to more effectively meet the needs of these hurting families. Even at that point, we never foresaw that God would call both of us to work for Abel Speaks full-time, but here we are. Since 2020, we have connected with nearly a hundred families across eighteen states, as well as Australia, England, and South Korea. One sweet mother recorded these words:

> I was sixteen weeks pregnant when my son received a life-limiting diagnosis. I remember being so afraid . . . afraid to lose him. Afraid to love him. Afraid of him. I cried thinking about all of my dreams slipping out of my hands, and then one night I came across Abel Speaks. I can remember the first time I saw a picture of Abel.

I can still so clearly remember that moment. Seeing his face changed my perspective. It was the first time I wasn't afraid of Ellis. God used his story to give me hope, and finally a breath of air, and I wasn't afraid. I was hopeful. We knew our baby boy was being knit together perfectly by his Creator for a purpose.

GOD USED HIS STORY TO GIVE ME HOPE, AND FINALLY A BREATH OF AIR, AND I WASN'T AFRAID. I WAS HOPEFUL.

Nothing will ever reverse the pain we feel from losing our baby boy. But Abel's life is not in vain, and God has not wasted an ounce of our pain. The sufferings entrusted to you are never for nothing. Christ suffered faithfully to bring us hope, and we suffer faithfully to spread his hope. Our mess can become a message, and our message can become a ministry, one person at a time.

1. **Why do you think so many stories of hardship and adversity resonate with us?** What is it that you see in the life of the sufferer that inspires you?

2. **Do you believe that God has entrusted you with a message in the midst of your suffering?** If so, what is that message? What would you hope to share with someone in your shoes?

3. **What are ways you can use your sorrow and journey to bless others in Christ?** How would you encourage others with what you have processed and learned recently?

4. **Finally, what are ways you have already seen one another embody the Gospel in your suffering thus far?** Affirm one another by sharing how your spouse has reminded you of Jesus along this difficult road.

1. **Take a moment to acknowledge** and articulate to God how the idea of "stewarding your suffering" makes you feel.

2. **If you can do so genuinely, invite God to help you embrace a "cruciform life" that reflects the Gospel to those around you.** If you're not there yet, pray that the days and weeks ahead will help move you closer to that and closer to him.

3. **Personalize and pray the following,** and feel encouraged to add anything else that you'd like to tell God. If you feel comfortable doing so, you could hold hands and do this together.

God, I confess that I resist the call to imitate the sufferings of Christ.

*I pray for your strength and your perspective,
especially in this season.*

I know you didn't waste Jesus' pain, and trust you won't waste mine.

*Thank you for the privilege of extending the hope of Christ to a
hurting world.*

Help me live a life shaped by the cross and for your glory.

One day at a time.

Amen.

THE PERSPECTIVE PURPOSE

"But you, keep your head in all situations, endure hardship, do the work of an evangelist, discharge all the duties of your ministry. For I am already being poured out like a drink offering, and the time for my departure is near. I have fought the good fight, I have finished the race, I have kept the faith. Now there is in store for me the crown of righteousness, which the Lord, the righteous Judge, will award to me on that day—and not only to me, but also to all who have longed for his appearing." —2 Timothy 4:5–8, emphasis added

We've spent this week exploring some of the biblical purposes of suffering. We may never know the exact reasons for our sorrows, but we *can* know without a doubt that our pain is never in vain. While God does not delight in it, we have seen that he does redeem it.

- Profoundly and mysteriously, he is able to use suffering for our good and our growth—to conform us increasingly to the image of Christ (Romans 8:28–29).

- We will know Jesus more deeply as we grow in our personal intimacy.

- We will follow Jesus more steadfastly as we grow in our spiritual maturity.

- We will represent Jesus more fully as we grow in our faithful ministry.

- And finally, we will see Jesus more clearly as we grow in our eternal perspective.

SCRIPTURE

"Since, then, you have been raised with Christ, set your hearts on things above, where Christ is, seated at the right hand of God. Set your minds on things above, not on earthly things. For you died, and your life is now hidden with Christ in God. When Christ, who is your life, appears, then you also will appear with him in glory." —Colossians 3:1–4

No single passage of Scripture has shaped and impacted us more over the past five years than the fourth chapter of Second Corinthians. I'd like to share its closing verses and spend the final day of our final week walking through it together:

> Therefore we do not lose heart. Though outwardly we are wasting away, yet inwardly we are being renewed day by day. For our light and momentary troubles are achieving for us an eternal glory that far outweighs them all. So we fix our eyes not on what is seen, but on what is unseen, since what is seen is temporary, but what is unseen is eternal (2 Corinthians 4:16–18).

LIGHT AND MOMENTARY

On its own, being told "don't lose heart" may not feel particularly helpful or hopeful. Why should I not lose heart in the midst of this affliction? How do I not lose heart when there is no clear end in sight? Paul shares his secrets with us, and the first reason given for not losing heart is that our worldly suffering is light and momentary.

Have you ever asked a woman in the middle of labor if the pain feels light and momentary? Not unless you want to get smacked. While women are unique in experiencing childbirth, everybody recognizes that the physical pain and mental fatigue can be almost unbearable. And yet, as new life is brought forth, the suffering is all worth it. In an instant, the joy of seeing and holding your child surpasses all the pain of pregnancy, labor, and delivery. So much so that the vast majority of moms will choose to have more children, voluntarily going through that process all over again. Think about that.

In the here and now, our suffering sure doesn't feel "light and momentary," does it? But as real and deep as the pain is, it will not outlive this present life which is like "a mist that appears for a little while

and then vanishes" (James 4:14b). These decades on earth are a tiny grain of sand on the endless seashore of eternity, where millions and billions of years of worshipping in the presence of God awaits. We can take heart because our hope is not in this world but in the world to come.

ENDURANCE AND ENJOYMENT

Speaking of the world to come, the next reason not to lose heart is that these afflictions are achieving for us an eternal weight of glory beyond all comparison and all comprehension. So our suffering isn't something we simply suck up and get through, like cosmic taxes paid prior to glory. No. Somehow, someway, our afflictions are actually helping produce that glory. Scripture is saying that there is a connection between our *endurance* of hardship now and our *enjoyment* of the glory of God in the ages to come.

If that sounds too ethereal and abstract, then consider the difference between seeing a picture from the top of Machu Picchu and physically standing on it. It's more than the photo resolution, it's about the ascent. The more breath is taken away (literally) on the way up, the more your breath will be taken away at the summit. No one would argue that a Google image search can match the beauty of personally experiencing Machu Picchu after you've pushed through the pain. It is beyond all comparison—not in spite of the difficult climb, but because of the difficult climb.

FIX YOUR EYES, DAY BY DAY

If that illustration rings true when reaching a Peruvian mountaintop, how much more will it ring true when reaching heaven and remaining there forever, and ever, and ever? Though we have no true concept of what it will be like, we know that none of the world's wonders can possibly do it justice. The closest thing we are given is John's vision in the penultimate chapter of our Bible. This is the "unseen and eternal" vision upon which Paul is exhorting us to fix our eyes.

Then I saw 'a new heaven and a new earth,' for the first heaven and the first earth had passed away, and there was no longer any sea. I saw the Holy City, the new Jerusalem, coming down out of heaven from God, prepared as a bride beautifully dressed for her husband. And I heard a loud voice from the throne saying, "Look! God's dwelling place is now among the people, and he will dwell with them. They will be his people, and God himself will be with them and be their God. 'He will wipe every tear from their eyes. There will be no more death' or mourning or crying or pain, for the old order of things has passed away."

He who was seated on the throne said, "I am making everything new!" Then he said, "Write this down, for these words are trustworthy and true." He said to me: "It is done. I am the Alpha and the Omega, the Beginning and the End. To the thirsty I will give water without cost from the spring of the water of life. Those who are victorious will inherit all this, and I will be their God and they will be my children" (Revelation 21:1–7).

The single most transformative means of not losing heart is to trade our worldly outlook for an eternal perspective. To fix our eyes not on what is seen and temporary, but on what is unseen and eternal. A new heaven and a new earth, unbroken by sin and suffering. God dwelling with us. No tears, no death, no mourning, and no pain. All things new, trustworthy and true. This is not some pipe dream rooted in wishful thinking. This is the promised future that awaits the children of God, reconciled to their Father through the suffering of his perfect Son.

Finally, we must remind ourselves of these truths "day by day" (2 Corinthians 4:16). We will never reach a point where we no longer need to fix our eyes on the unseen. We need these regular rhythms of remembrance because we are so prone to wander and quick to forget. If we desire to take heart and to be renewed, we must do so one day at a time. Day by day, hour by hour, moment by moment. We will never graduate from this. No book or workbook will suffice. No change in circumstances will suffice. A daily, consistent, personal, devoted walk with Christ is the only way. Take heart, one day at a time, for he has overcome the world (John 16:33).

THE SINGLE MOST TRANSFORMATIVE MEANS OF NOT LOSING HEART IS TO TRADE OUR WORLDLY OUTLOOK FOR AN ETERNAL PERSPECTIVE.

1. **Reread 2 Corinthians 4:16–18 from the beginning of the lesson.** What part of that passage resonates or stands out to you the most?

2. **How does the notion that your suffering is "light and momentary" sound at first hearing?** Hurtful? Hopeful? Neither?

3. **We mentioned childbirth and mountain climbing, but are there other examples where hardship leads us to something greater that feels "worth it"?** Can you think of any personal experiences from your own life?

4. **Does the hope of heaven feel more real or less real to you than before this season of suffering?** Up to this point, have you ever taken time to intentionally "fix your eyes on the unseen"?

5. **Given that it's the final day of this workbook, how will you continue this rhythm of walking with God and meditating on his Word "day by day"?** Start by choosing a time, a place, and a reading plan. Encourage one another and hold each other accountable. Don't let this be the end of the road!

1. **Take a moment to acknowledge** and articulate to God if you are having difficulty taking your eyes off of your sufferings and onto your Savior.

2. **If you can do so genuinely, ask God for the perspective to truly see your sufferings as "light and momentary" compared to eternity with him.** If you're not there yet, pray that the days and weeks ahead will help move you closer to that and closer to him.

3. **Personalize and pray the following,** and feel encouraged to add anything else that you'd like to tell God. If you feel comfortable doing so, you could hold hands and do this together.

God, I don't want to lose heart.

While I'm outwardly wasting away, you can renew my heart each day.

Thank you for the unbelievable hope of heaven and eternity with you.

Help me believe that these hardships are light and momentary in comparison.

Help me look beyond my sufferings and fix my heart and mind on the unseen.

One day at a time.

Amen.

"

If we desire to take heart and to be renewed, we must do so one day at a time. Day by day, hour by hour, moment by moment.

abel SPEAKS

Daniel and Kelly Crawford co-founded Abel Speaks in 2018 to support families who have chosen to carry a child with a life-limiting diagnosis. After walking that road with their firstborn son, Abel, they realized the significant need that existed for parents in their position.

The vision of Abel Speaks is that every family they serve will cherish their child's life and have hope in the midst of sorrow. This ministry is but one example of the redemptive truth that God never wastes an ounce of our pain.

GO TO ABELSPEAKS.ORG TO FIND OUT MORE.

Even if . . .

"If we are thrown into the blazing furnace, the God we serve is able to deliver us from it, and he will deliver us from Your Majesty's hand. But even if he does not, we want you to know, Your Majesty, that we will not serve your gods or worship the image of gold you have set up."

—DANIEL 3:17–18

Let us be the first to say congratulations on completing this workbook!

We pray you might look back on these past four weeks as a turning point in your faith and a turning point in your focus. New eyes, a new lens, and a new perspective through which you view the troubles of this life. Looking beyond our present pain, and looking ahead to our future inheritance through him. Discovering that our eternal vision will outweigh our current affliction. Slowly but surely, one day at a time.

We'd like to leave you with some words we wrote to our incredible support network the day before Abel was born as a "line in the sand" sort of declaration:

> On the eve of Abel's birth, we want to clearly communicate that we believe God is good, faithful, and trustworthy—*even if* we do not find Abel physically healed tomorrow as we've been praying. Rather than an "*if-then*" faith filled with conditions and contingencies, we believe that followers of Christ are called to an "*even if*" faith (Daniel 3:16–18) that unconditionally honors and clings to a faithful God in every scenario. We don't know what tomorrow has in store, and in that regard it's still really scary for us to think about. But we know that as followers of Jesus, redeemed by his own sufferings, we declare today, 'I have chosen the way of faithfulness, and I have set my heart on your ways' (Psalm 119:30). We take heart in the eternal hope we have through our suffering Savior, who gave his earthly life that we may truly live with him, forever. It's been quite a journey so far. Thank you for being with us every step of the way. We love you.

After spending a month prioritizing and pursuing your walk with God as you walk through suffering, we hope you will consider drawing your own line in the sand, declaring that you will follow God no matter what the future holds.

WE LOVE YOU,
DANIEL & KELLY CRAWFORD

christian parenting

PERFECTLY. IMPERFECT.

We want to be better parents. We want to give our children the love and attention they need. But our lives are so busy, and we're stretched so thin, that it can be hard to do more than the status quo.

So we created Christian Parenting to give parents everywhere the practical and spiritual help they need, on as many platforms as possible.

With the right resources given to you in the right ways, growth can happen in the midst of the busyness. You don't need to be perfect. In fact, growth comes as you embrace becoming perfectly imperfect.

Go to **ChristianParenting.org** to find out how.

NOTES

Introduction

    11   **"the state of undergoing pain":** "Suffering definition," Lexico, https://www.lexico.com/en/definition/suffering.

    11   **"suffering is having what you don't":** Elisabeth Elliot, *A Path through Suffering* (Grand Rapids: Baker Publishing Group, 2014).

Week 1

    Day 3

    28   **"God will either give us":** Timothy Keller, Prayer: *Experiencing Awe and Intimacy with God* (New York: Penguin Books, 2016).

    29   **"Just pray what you got.":** Matt Chandler, "Practicing Prayer" (sermon), September 15, 2019.

Week 2

    45   **The book is called When Helping Hurts:** Steve Corbett and Brian Fikkert, *When Helping Hurts: How to Alleviate Poverty Without Hurting the Poor . . . and Yourself* (Chicago: Moody Publishers, 2014).

    Day 1

    47   **"Jesus used the term blessed":** "What Does It Mean to be Blessed?," Got Questions Ministries, accessed July 1, 2020, https://www.gotquestions.org/mean-to-be-blessed.html.

    Day 2

    52   **simplified definition for suffering:** Elliot Elisabeth and Joni Eareckson Tada, *Suffering Is Never for Nothing* (Nashville: B&H Publishing Group, 2019).

    Day 5

    67   **"As we continue to walk":** Anne Ungarean, "The Deepest Water, The Purest Well," Abel Speaks, March 24, 2020, https://www.abelspeaks.org/blog/deepestwell.

Week 3

    Day 2

    82   **a weekly check-in with each other:** Connie Dunn, "Today's Letters 5 Weekly Questions," Kindred Events Studio, December 10, 2013, http://kindredeventstudio.com/blog/2013/12/9/todays-letters-5-weekly-questions.

    Day 5

    96   **the classic hymn:** Helen Howart Lemmel, "Turn Your Eyes Upon Jesus," 1922, https://www.hymnal.net/en/hymn/h/645.

Week 4

    Day 4

    121   **"I was sixteen weeks pregnant":** "Abel Speaks: Story and Vision," YouTube, October 4, 2019, www.youtube.com/watch?v=qLJrbTZpQB8. Accessed 29 July 2020.